Classroom Management for All Teachers

Plans for Evidence-Based Practice

TEACHER PREP

MERRILL
PRENTICE HALL

Teacher Preparation Classroom

See a demo at
www.prenhall.com/teacherprep/demo

Your Class. Their Careers. Our Future. Will your students be prepared?

We invite you to explore our new, innovative and engaging website and all that it has to offer you, your course, and tomorrow's educators! Preview this site today at www.prenhall.com/teacherprep/demo. Just click on "go" on the login page to begin your exploration.

Organized around the major courses pre-service teachers take, the Teacher Preparation site provides media, student/teacher artifacts, strategies, research articles, and other resources to equip your students with the quality tools needed to excel in their courses and prepare them for their first classroom.

This ultimate online education resource will provide you and your students access to:

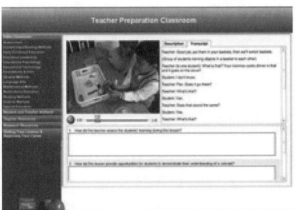

Online Video Library. More than 250 video clips—each tied to a course topic and framed by learning goals and Praxis-type questions—capture real teachers and students working in real classrooms.

Student and Teacher Artifacts. More than 200 student and teacher classroom artifacts—each tied to a course topic and framed by learning goals and application questions—provide a wealth of materials and experiences to help your students observe children's developmental learning.

Lesson Plan Builder. Step-by-step guidelines and lesson plan examples support students as they learn to build high-quality lesson plans.

Articles and Readings. Over 500 articles from ASCD's renowned journal *Educational Leadership* are available. The site also includes Research Navigator, a searchable database of additional educational journals.

Strategies and Lessons. Over 500 research-supported instructional strategies appropriate for a wide range of grade levels and content areas.

Licensure and Career Tools. Resources devoted to helping your students pass their licensure exam; learn standards, law, and public policies; plan a teaching portfolio; and succeed in their first year of teaching.

How to ORDER *Teacher Prep* for you and your students:
For students to receive a *Teacher Prep* Access Code with this text, instructors **must** provide a special value pack ISBN number on their textbook order form. To receive this special ISBN, please email
Merrill.marketing@pearsoned.com and provide the following information:
- Name and Affiliation
- Author/Title/Edition of Merrill text

Upon ordering *Teacher Prep* for their students, instructors will be given a lifetime *Teacher Prep* Access Code.

Classroom Management for All Teachers

Plans for Evidence-Based Practice

Third Edition

ENNIO CIPANI

National University

Upper Saddle River, New Jersey
Columbus, Ohio

Library of Congress Cataloging in Publication Data

Cipani, Ennio.
  Classroom management for all teachers: plans for evidence-based
practice / Ennio Cipani.—3rd ed.
      p. cm.
  Includes bibliographical references.
  ISBN 0-13-199164-7 (pbk., perforated)
  1. Classroom management—United States—Handbooks, manuals, etc.
  2. School discipline—United States—Handbooks, manuals, etc. I. Title.
  LB3013.C514 2008
  371.102′4—dc22

                                                    2006027561

Vice President and Executive Publisher: Jeffery W. Johnston
Executive Editor: Ann Castel Davis
Editorial Assistant: Penny S. Burleson
Senior Production Editor: Linda Hillis Bayma
Production Coordination: Thistle Hill Publishing Services, LLC
Design Coordinator: Diane C. Lorenzo
Cover Designer: Ali Mohrman
Cover image: Reflected ceiling plan of a vaulted archway in the Palazzo Della
    Cancellaria, Rome (1486) by architect Donato Bramante (1444–1514)
Production Manager: Laura Messerly
Director of Marketing: David Gesell
Marketing Manager: Autumn Purdy
Marketing Coordinator: Brian Mounts

This book was set in Dutch 823 BT by Integra Software Services. It was printed and bound by Bind-Rite Graphics.
The cover was printed by Phoenix Color Corp.

Pearson Education Ltd.   Pearson Education Australia Pty. Limited
Pearson Education Singapore Pte. Ltd. Pearson Education North Asia Ltd.
Pearson Education Canada, Ltd.   Pearson Educación de Mexico, S.A. de C.V.
Pearson Education—Japan   Pearson Education Malaysia Pte. Ltd.

10 9 8 7 6 5 4
ISBN-13: 978-0-13-199164-4
ISBN-10:   0-13-199164-7

About the Author

Ennio Cipani is a full professor in the Department of Special Education and Technology at National University, Fresno Academic Center (e-mail is ecipani@nu.edu). He previously held positions at the California School of Professional Psychology in the child clinical doctoral psychology program (1993–2005) and was a faculty member at the University of the Pacific in the Department of Special Education (1981–1993, the last 3 years as the department chair). He graduated from Florida State University with a Ph.D. in educational psychology. He has published many articles, chapters, and books on child behavior management, including *Helping Parents Help Their Kids: A Clinical Guide to Six Child Problem Behaviors*, *Non-compliance: Four Strategies That Work*, and *Disruptive Behavior*. He has developed a 4-hour CD training package titled "A Functional Analysis of Behavior Model for School Settings." He has been a licensed psychologist in private practice in California since 1983, primarily training parents and teachers in specific, individually tailored behavior management plans for children with severe behavior problems in the home and school.

Preface

Many school personnel turn to behavioral plans and programs when a child's behavior has become extremely problematic. Certainly, behavioral management plans are well suited in extreme circumstances to change behavior problems by developing more appropriate behavior in children with severe behavior problems. The research base is replete with examples of validated management strategies. But one should not conclude that these plans are of use only in these dire circumstances. I have often heard teachers say, "Oh, his behavior isn't bad enough to warrant a behavioral plan." This equating of behavior plans as appropriate only for severe levels of problem behaviors has been perpetuated by misguided people, and nothing could be further from the truth!

Instead, one should look at the use of these plans as good prevention. An effective classwide behavior management system will probably prevent small problems from becoming bigger problems, and moderate-size problems from creating a disaster. Systematic behavioral management is not just for treatment; it is also good prevention.

CONTENTS OF THIS TEXT

This teacher manual presents user-friendly information on 10 classroom management plans, derived from an empirical research basis, for use with individual children or entire classes.

Management plans are detailed for two common problem areas:

1. Disruptive behavior and rule violations
2. On-task and assignment completion problems

Like the second edition, this third edition provides teachers with specific plans of classroom management. The third edition continues the tradition of maintaining the scientific nature of these plans; hence the term *evidence-based practice*. Part 1 delineates evidence-based treatment and how this methodology applies to education and learning. The plans described in the last two parts of this book have a basis in behavior analysis classroom management research. This research base serves as the "clinical trials" methodology for understanding the efficacy of behavioral management systems in changing student behavior.

Disruptive behavior and rule violations are addressed in part 2. Two new plans have been added to the third edition in this section. The Good Behavior Board Game, a variation of the previous edition's Good Behavior Game, has several new features that warrant close attention. In particular, the use of a board game format across the entire class makes this new version easier and more feasible for teachers to implement. Two board mazes are included in the forms section. A new plan, Positive Compliance Momentum, which addresses the host of problems that some teachers face during activity transitions, is included in this edition.

Part 3 contains four management plans designed to increase student on-task behavior. If a teacher can develop a strategy that increases the student's engagement in task materials and teacher-presented instruction, other behavior problems will often greatly decrease. When children are *engaged* in tasks and academic instruction, there is less opportunity to engage in other (unacceptable) behavior. It is strongly recommended that teachers become familiar with the plans contained in part 3 and apply them frequently, both to prevent potential problems and to solve current problem behaviors. In particular, the beeper system is a powerful program for enhancing student engagement, with the aid of a device called the MotivAider.

PRESENTATION FORMAT OF EACH MANAGEMENT PLAN IN PARTS 2 AND 3

This manual uses a uniform format to present each classroom management plan:

1. Brief description of plan
2. Terms
3. Apparatus
4. Baseline measurement
5. Procedures
6. How it works
7. Additional considerations
8. Hypothetical example(s)
9. What if?
10. Forms

WHO CAN USE THIS MANUAL?

This manual is well suited for current and prospective teachers, as both a resource and a preservice teaching tool. It provides in-depth coverage of specific classroom behavioral management plans for individual students (e.g., Individual Disruptive Incident Barometer) as well as systems for entire classrooms (Good Behavior Board Game). It is written in a nontechnical style, free of most "behavioral" jargon. One need not have extensive training in behavior therapy or learning theory to understand how to apply any of the techniques presented in this manual in their basic form. Obviously, developing variations of these techniques for unique circumstances may require additional training through courses in behavior analysis and field supervision from personnel specializing in applied behavior analysis.

This supplemental manual can be used in a variety of university undergraduate and graduate courses. It is used for teacher training programs, as well as in-service training, because it describes specific applications for classroom management systems for K–12 grade levels. It therefore serves an often-needed bridge from theory to practice. Auto mechanics, cooks, and hospital administrators, as well as other technical and professional personnel, all have manuals detailing procedures in their everyday tasks. Now teachers and school psychologists also have a manual.

For the following university courses, I believe this *supplemental text* would be useful in the particular course as described below.

Classroom Management Courses (General or Special Education Departments)

Many primary texts may not provide enough detail on how to design a classroom management system. As a supplement to a primary text, this manual can focus on specific applications of a classroom management system to general education and special education classes. In that regard, the management systems that should be covered are the Good Behavior Board Game, the Beeper System, the Task Engagement Program, and Response Cards. These systems can all be used classwide and constitute good preventative strategies. The Good Behavior Board Game in particular can be effectively used in large general education classes and special day classes (mild to moderate disabilities). Response Cards is an effective instructional and behavior management system, and students should become familiar with its use in various academic content areas.

Behavior Management Courses

This text effectively demonstrates the application of behavioral principles to managing a classroom. Whereas the primary text in a behavior management course may present the principles of reinforcement, the plans in this book illustrate the use of these principles in the classroom. For example, one of the behavioral concepts covered in a primary text might be the Premack Principle. A specific application of the Premack Principle, Grandma's Rule for Increasing In-Seat Behavior, is described in this text. This plan is applicable when the teacher needs to increase the amount of time a child stays in his/her seat.

Special Education Methods Courses

Classroom management topics can often be partially covered in methods courses. However, the time spent on this topic in methods courses is often shorter than is needed for students to acquire sufficient skills. With this supplemental text, teachers can assign readings to the students on real-life applications for managing classrooms. Therefore, students will be provided a few tools for classroom management without taking away valuable class time. Students should focus on the plans for classwide systems (see classroom management courses above). Response Cards is an effective instructional and behavior management system and should be developed in a methods course as an adjunct to other instructional methods.

Consultation Courses (Special Education and School Psychology)

School consultants evaluate individual students with behavioral problems. While I believe it is important for them to be familiar with classwide strategies, the focus of study in this course should be on individual applications. This is particularly true in light of the federal requirement for implementing evidence-based positive behavioral intervention plans. The plans that should be covered in this course are Grandma's Rule for Increasing In-Seat Behavior, Response Cards (used in an individual or small group application), Behavioral Contracting, Individual Disruptive Incident Barometer, and Positive Compliance Momentum.

Inclusion Courses

For students being educated in inclusive settings, problem behaviors can often hinder a student's success. General and special education teachers should have skills in developing individual behavior management plans that allow a student to become more successful in inclusive environments. In particular, Behavioral Contracting, the Individual Disruptive Incident Barometer, Positive Compliance Momentum, Signal Time-out, the Beeper System, and Grandma's Rule for Increasing In-Seat Behavior should be requisite skills for all teachers involved in the education of special needs students.

Educational Psychology Courses (Undergrad and Grad)

In an introductory course in educational psychology, application can often be a missing component. The use of this supplemental text can certainly bring life to a discussion of applying basic principles of behavior to real-life problems. My recommendation is to present one or more plans involving classwide systems (e.g., Task Engagement Program, Good Behavior Board Game), as well as plans that focus on individual student application (e.g., Behavioral Contracting, Individual Disruptive Incident Barometer).

Student Teaching/Fieldwork

The applications in this manual make it well suited as a stand-alone text for student teaching. Supervisors can consult with the student teacher on specific students and individual behavior management programs or the use of classwide systems. Using the forms during fieldwork makes the student teacher begin to appreciate the need for documentation, particularly in special education.

Applied Behavior Analysis/Behavior Modification Courses (Psychology)

This text can serve as an outstanding supplement to courses in applied behavior analysis/behavior modification. The detailed management plans can provide students in these courses with the application of basic principles of human behavior as they apply to school settings.

NEW FEATURES IN THE THIRD EDITION

Knowledge Competency Tests and Certificates of Competence

A unique feature of the third edition allows for an objective measure of competency with respect to a student's understanding of the 10 plans contained herein. For each plan, a 6–13 item test can be downloaded from the Prentice Hall Instructor Resource Center (www.prenhall.com) by the faculty member or in-service training personnel. To achieve knowledge competence, the student must achieve an 80% correct response level. A certificate of competence can be provided to the student from the faculty member or site administrator, listing those plans for which the student has achieved a mastery level of knowledge competence. This requirement can be made part of the class or an option, depending on the course and instructor preference.

I believe that, in this era of the No Child Left Behind (NCLB) Act and concomitant accountability, providing students with an objective assessment of their understanding of these empirically derived plans needs to be a requisite in teacher training. I hope this unique competency-based testing component is welcomed by university faculty as well as by in-service training personnel and administrators. For university training programs, I believe it will provide a competitive edge for your graduates. Passing these competency tests can verify to prospective employers during interviews that your graduates have certain specific skills in classroom management systems. A graduate from a university program in computer science can demonstrate proficiency in programming languages. Now, prospective teachers and school psychologists can also verify knowledge of specific behavior management programs. Students who leave your course can be given a copy of the certificate of competence that lists the management plan(s) in which they have achieved knowledge competency.

For in-service training and professional development personnel, having a substantial number of on-site teachers trained in specific classroom management systems may serve several purposes. Accreditation agencies and the public may view such a capability as a positive step for schools to take in addressing NCLB. Second, the competent use of such systems can have a significant effect on discipline problems and improved school atmosphere. A certificate of competency is also available for professional development personnel and/or the site administrator's use for teachers who pass the competency test(s). It may be a measure of excellence for your school or district to present such certificates to accrediting agencies and/or the consuming public.

I suggest that university faculty and in-service training specialists allow students/teachers to take only one or two competency tests at a time. It may be difficult for the test-taking individuals to keep all the distinctive features of each plan in mind when taking a longer series of tests. The competency tests measure the person's knowledge of the procedural aspects of the plan. I do not believe there are any trick questions. The tests do provide a measurement of student understanding of the procedural aspects of each management plan.

Two New Management Plans

This third edition includes two new plans. The Good Behavior Board Game is a variation of the Good Behavior Game from the previous edition. In this edition, the game is played with the classroom as an entire team, making it easier for the teacher to conduct. Further, more ancillary materials are included in this edition to accommodate the board game aspect, including two game mazes in the forms section.

A difficult area for some teachers is activity transitions. This edition includes a plan that addresses activity transitions called Positive Compliance Momentum. With this technique, teachers develop a momentum of student compliance to teachers' instructions using simple behaviors before presenting the activity transition request(s) to the class. It is particularly suited for students in the lower grade levels.

Behavioral Consultation to School Personnel (Appendix B)

The plans contained in this book are useful for personnel who provide indirect services as well. Special education personnel and school psychologists are frequently asked to consult on individual cases involving students with behavioral problems. Student study teams often deal with children being considered for referral as a primary (or secondary) result of their behavior. Appendix B in this third edition addresses how consultants can use these plans to help teachers who serve children with behavior problems in special education and/or inclusive settings. This is especially important in light of the requirement for children in special education who exhibit behavior problems because it is required that they have an individual positive behavioral intervention plan designed for them. Appendix B provides a data-driven model of consultation for problem behaviors in all educational settings.

A Downloaded Streaming Audiovisual Slide Presentation (of First Chapter)

For faculty adopting this supplemental text or for professional development personnel using this text for in-service training, an audiovisual slide show is available from the Prentice Hall Instructor Resource Center (www.prenhall.com). This slide show presents a 20-minute lecture on the first chapter, which describes the use of evidence-based procedures in classroom management. It can be played during class as part of the lecture or downloaded to a CD and stored in a resource library for students to check out (and return). It contains 14 slides with an accompanying lecture from the author of this text.

ACKNOWLEDGMENTS

I wish to thank the following reviewers for their useful comments and understanding of the scope and intention of this material: Deborah Hartman, Cedar Crest College; Gerald Ketterling, Benedictine University; Sharon A. Lynch, Sam Houston State University; and Annette C. Robinson, Seattle Pacific University.

Discover the Merrill Resources for Special Education Website

Technology is a constantly growing and changing aspect of our field that is creating a need for new content and resources. To address this emerging need, Merrill Education has developed an online learning environment for students, teachers, and professors alike to complement our products—the *Merrill Resources for Special Education* Website. This content-rich website provides additional resources specific to this book's topic and will help you—professors, classroom teachers, and students—augment your teaching, learning, and professional development.

Our goal is to build on and enhance what our products already offer. For this reason, the content for our user-friendly website is organized by topic and provides teachers, professors, and students with a variety of meaningful resources all in one location. With this website, we bring together the best of what Merrill has to offer: text resources, video clips, web links, tutorials, and a wide variety of information on topics of interest to general and special educators alike. Rich content, applications, and competencies further enhance the learning process.

The *Merrill Resources for Special Education* Website includes:

- Video clips specific to each topic, with questions to help you evaluate the content and make crucial theory-to-practice connections.
- Thought-provoking critical analysis questions that students can answer and turn in for evaluation or that can serve as basis for class discussions and lectures.
- Access to a wide variety of resources related to classroom strategies and methods, including lesson planning and classroom management.
- Information on all the most current relevant topics related to special and general education, including CEC and Praxis™ standards, IEPs, portfolios, and professional development.
- Extensive web resources and overviews on each topic addressed on the website.
- A search feature to help access specific information quickly.

To take advantage of these and other resources, please visit the *Merrill Resources for Special Education* Website at **http://www.prenhall.com/cipani**

Contents

PART 1

Introduction to Classroom Management for All Teachers: Evidence-Based Practice   1

1 Classroom Management and Evidence-Based Practice   5

What Is Evidence-Based Practice?   6

The Imperative for Evidence-Based Practice   7

Research Proof: Building a Better Mousetrap (Pardon the Pun)   11

Who Needs Evidence-Based Procedures?   13

    Teacher Challenge 1: Dealing with Extremely Aggressive and Disruptive Students   13

    Teacher Challenge 2: Daily Encounters with Disruptive Behavior   16

    Teacher Challenge 3: Unmotivated Students   18

Punished by Rewards? I Don't Think So!   19

Wanted: Intrinsically Motivated Students   22

Developing Competent Learners: The Case for Intrinsic Motivation   25

PART 2

Plans for Reducing or Eliminating Disruptive and Rule-Violation Behavior   27

2 The Good Behavior Board Game   31

Brief Description   32

Terms   32

Apparatus   33

Baseline Measurement   33

Procedures   34

How It Works   35

Additional Considerations   36

Children Who Are More Disruptive Than Others   36

*Provide Intermittent Praise for Nondisruptive
Behavior   36*

Hypothetical Example   37

*Use of a Classwide Good Behavior Board Game for a
Tenth-Grade Math Class   37*

What If?   38

Forms   38

3 Behavioral Contracting   55

Brief Description   56

Terms   56

Apparatus   56

Baseline Measurement   57

Procedures   57

How It Works   58

Additional Considerations   58

Inaccurate Baseline Data   58

Strengthen Reinforcers   58

Application for Aggressive Behavior   59

Hypothetical Example   59

Dealing with Physical Aggression   59

Hypothetical Example   60

Increasing Appropriate Behavior   60

What If?   60

Forms   61

4 Individual Disruptive Incident Barometer   69

Brief Description   70

Terms   70

Apparatus   70

Baseline Measurement   71

Procedures   71

How It Works   72

Additional Considerations   72

When a Child Falls Below the Barometer Line   72

Inaccurate Baseline Data   73

Strengthen Reinforcers   73

Hypothetical Example   73
    Reducing Teasing   73
What If?   74
Forms   74

5 Signal Time-Out for Minor Disruptive Behavior   79

Brief Description   80
Terms   80
Apparatus   80
Baseline Measurement   80
Procedures   80
How It Works   81
Additional Considerations   81
    Setting a Minimum Signal Time-Out Length   81
    Altering the Density of Beeps on the Beeper System   82
Hypothetical Example   82
    Group Application for "Chatter"   82
What If?   82
Forms   82

6 Removal Time-Out for Severe Disruptive and Aggressive Behavior   87

Brief Description   88
Terms   88
Apparatus   88
Baseline Measurement   88
Procedures   89
How It Works   89
Additional Consideration   89
Hypothetical Example   90
    Removal Time-Out for Verbal Abuse   90
What If?   90
Forms   90

7 Positive Compliance Momentum   99

Brief Description   100
Terms   100
Apparatus   101
Baseline Measurement   101
Procedures   101
How It Works   102

Additional Considerations   102

Use the Good Behavior Board Game as an Additional Component   102

Standardize the Transition Routine   103

Hypothetical Example   103

"Simon Says"   103

What If?   104

Form   104

PART 3

Plans for Keeping on Task and Completing Assignments   107

8   The Beeper System   111

Brief Description   112

Terms   112

Apparatus   112

Baseline Measurement   114

Procedures   115

How It Works   115

Additional Considerations   116

Appointing a Chart Manager   116

Keeping Up with the Beeper System   116

Monitoring Performance in Groups   116

Teaching Students to Self-Monitor   117

Low Performers   117

Increasing the Behavior Standard   118

Gradually Reducing the "Density" of Beeps   118

A "Graded" System for Earning Reinforcement   118

Hypothetical Example   119

Two Low-Performing Target Students   119

Hypothetical Example   119

High School American History   120

What If?   121

Forms   121

9   Task Engagement Program (TEP)   133

Brief Description   134

Terms   134

Apparatus   135

Baseline Measurement   135

Procedures   136

How It Works   137

Additional Considerations   137

   Appointing a Star Chart Manager   137

   Teaching Students to Self-Monitor   137

   Shaping Task Engagement   138

   Increasing the Behavior Standard   138

   A "Graded" System for Earning Reinforcement   138

Hypothetical Example   139

   Classwide Implementation of the TEP   139

What If?   139

Forms   140

10 Grandma's Rule for Increasing In-Seat Behavior   149

Brief Description   150

Terms   150

Apparatus   151

Baseline Measurement   151

Procedures   151

How It Works   152

Additional Consideration   153

   Implementing the Program with One Student at a Time   153

Hypothetical Example   153

   Increasing Sitting During Story Time   153

What If?   153

Forms   154

11 Response Cards   163

Brief Description   164

Terms   164

Apparatus   164

Procedures   165

How It Works   165

Additional Consideration   166

   Designing Test Items for "Chunks"   166

Hypothetical Example   166

   Use of Response Cards in Algebra I class   166

What If?   167

Contents

Epilogue   169

Appendix A
   Using Powerful Reinforcers in Your Classroom   171

Appendix B
   Providing Behavioral Consultation to School Personnel   177

References   185

PART 1

Introduction to Classroom Management for All Teachers: Evidence-Based Practice

Chapter 1
Classroom Management and Evidence-Based Practice

The classroom challenges facing teachers today are many. The behavior of students in today's classrooms is reported to be more unruly, and more frequently unruly, than in prior decades (Miller, 1996). The reasons given as contributing factors for this state of affairs are varied, ranging from parental irresponsibility to new teaching methods and philosophies (Miller, 1996). Often, the causal factors cited for the decay of appropriate behaviors in many children attending public school classrooms are events beyond the control of teachers, such as the rising number of dysfunctional parents, two-parent working families, children raised by grandparents, and a variety of societal problems. Many school personnel come to believe they cannot help some of the students because of these endemic societal problems. If they are to help them, school personnel feel they need to "fix" those problems by taking on other roles. It is no wonder that teachers feel overwhelmed on the job.

Is it the case that teaching children 4 decades ago was simply a matter of presenting lessons, without having to deal with discipline problems on an hourly or more frequent basis? Do students today come to public education not ready to learn and profit from the instruction? If it is more difficult to manage the behavior of students in classrooms today, what is needed?

There is an approach that can provide help to teachers in managing student behavior in the classroom. An empirical research base, demonstrating the effectiveness of certain procedures with problems and issues in managing students in classrooms, has been in existence for over 4 decades. The field of applied behavior analysis has produced many studies on classroom management since the 1960s. I believe the imperative to adopt a position regarding the use of evidence-based procedures has never been more compelling than it is today. Evidence-based practice should be performed by all teachers. Perhaps this real-life case will illustrate how evidence-based practice can be used for students that can be extremely difficult to handle.

Can Anything Help Steve?

Steve[1] was 9 years old, attending an elementary school in a rural area of California. He spent half his day in third grade and the other half in a resource room. He displayed extreme behavioral difficulties, including refusal to do work and aggression toward teachers, the principal, and other children. He was expelled as a result of an incident in which he physically assaulted his third-grade teacher and the principal. Steve was diagnosed with major depression and posttraumatic stress disorder. He was placed on Prozac as a medication treatment for his problems and was also attending counseling sessions with a therapist. Maybe children like Steve were only fictional characters in the 1950s theater, but this story is nonfiction in the late 1990s.

Steve and his family had been involved with Child Protective Services (CPS) as a result of family turmoil. Steve was also rebellious in the home. As a result of a number of incidents involving neglect and physical abuse, he was detained by CPS. He was placed in a foster home but quickly proved to be a nightmare for his foster family. After a short stay, the foster mother called CPS during one of his outbursts. While she was on the phone with the emergency on-call person, Steve began to rant and scream profanities. When he reportedly threatened to "kill the family," the police were called and he was moved to a psychiatric hospital.

---

[1] All cases described in the text have altered identifying information to protect the confidentiality of the individuals.

It soon became apparent that Steve would not comply with any regimen. At the psychiatric hospital, his behavior became increasingly more difficult to deal with. He often argued and fought with staff and the other patients, and he was placed in isolation on many occasions. The attending physician felt that there was no other alternative.

He was discharged from the hospital as a result of their evaluation of his progress—there was none. The hospital staff felt they could not handle him, so CPS was forced to take him back. With no other place for Steve to go, CPS returned him to his father and mother. This news eventually reached the school district, and the phrase "He's back" must have occurred to the teachers and administrators.

It was unlikely that Steve would return to the school. His aggression to the teachers and students in the class made his return a safety issue. He was afforded an hour a day of home instruction with his resource specialist teacher and a psychiatric technician from the Department of Mental Health.

Steve's home instruction did not proceed well. Every day the teacher and a psychiatric technician (called psych tech) would show up at the house. The teacher would take out the assignments for the 1-hour period, as well as the homework, and present the material to Steve. Steve would then usually refuse to do such work (without assault at this point). The teacher would wait a period of time. If Steve did not engage in the assignment, she would leave early, usually within the first 10 to 20 minutes of arriving. I was called into the case to develop a behavioral plan to address his defiance. What could be done to motivate Steve to complete his assignments? Obviously, waiting for him to get the "urge to learn" was not an effective strategy. I would need to identify a powerful incentive that could compete with his unwillingness to perform his assignments. This reinforcer would have to be something that he could not get from home or friends, so as to not allow anyone to subvert the plan.

The answer came when the resource teacher relayed to me that Steve had always liked his first-grade teacher, Mrs. Falon. She indicated that he had very few problems when he was a first-grade student. In fact, prior to being removed from home and while he was still attending school, he would sometimes go to Mrs. Falon's class during school hours or after hours and help the first-grade students with their class assignments. As soon as the resource teacher said this, I knew I found my answer. A program I designed for noncompliance called the Compliance Barometer Program (Cipani, 1999) would be suitable.

I would make Steve's access to helping the first-grade class contingent on his performing his assignments for the hour-long home instruction period. It was a very simple plan. Each time he completed all his assignments during home instruction, he would be given a star for that day. His assignments for the hour were written on a task chart, with three or four tasks assigned per day. Each assignment that he completed was checked by the teacher. When he had accumulated four stars, he was given a pass to go the following day (or shortly thereafter) to school to spend an hour in Mrs. Falon's class (with one psych tech in tow). Steve would have to follow the rules established by Mrs. Falon, lest he lose (for the remainder of the time period) his privilege to be a class helper.

Within the first 3 weeks and after some mistakes in implementation and a curriculum mismatch were straightened out, success came. Steve was reliably earning his stars and getting to help in the first-grade class. He did not misbehave even once when he was in Mrs. Falon's class. His progress was so remarkable that the resource teacher broached the subject with me to bring him back to her classroom trailer. We agreed that he could do this for 1 hour and that he would be there at a time when other children were not scheduled.

Within a month of beginning his on-site school program, he was working several hours in the trailer with other children in attendance with no incidents (i.e., no aggressive behavior toward peers or teacher and no extreme outbursts). The resource teacher was delighted with his progress and indicated that next year she would transition him into a full-day program, with hopes of getting him back into regular education in areas in which he was within range of the general curriculum. Everyone was elated that we had succeeded in turning this child around and that he was now benefiting from an educational program.

1

Classroom Management and Evidence-Based Practice

WHAT IS EVIDENCE-BASED PRACTICE?

The behavioral strategy used for Steve was based on procedures validated in the applied behavior analysis research field over the past 4 decades (Abramowitz & O'Leary, 1991; Brooks, Todd, Tofflemeyer, & Horner, 2003; Kazdin, 1977; O'Leary & Drabman, 1971; O'Leary & O'Leary, 1977; Pigott & Heggie, 1986; West et al., 1995). The field of applied behavior analysis has tested behavioral management systems since the 1960s and early 1970s (Barrish, Saunders, & Wolf, 1969; Becker, Madsen, Arnold, & Thomas, 1967; Greenwood, Hops, Delquadri, & Guild, 1974; O'Leary, Becker, Evans, & Saudargas, 1969). Everyday practice is driven by procedures that have been found effective for various problems. Perhaps an example from another professional field will help portray the characteristics of evidence-based practice.

A physician prescribes a treatment regimen of insulin injections and blood sugar monitoring for a patient with diabetes. Is this regimen prescribed simply because the physician has a strong feeling that it will work or because it is based on sound theory? Neither! The use of insulin for certain diabetic patients is prescribed because of the prior extensive clinical testing of the treatment with diabetic patients. Evidence-based practice is the use of treatments or strategies that have received empirical support as being effective for the symptoms or problems of a given target population. In other words, there is a scientific basis for using a treatment for a certain disorder (Drake et al., 2001; Millenson, 1997).

Evidence-based practitioners are professionals who rely on scientific studies that have validated a treatment as having a high success rate in solving the presenting problem. The evidence-based practitioner does not actually conduct such scientific studies but is a consumer of science. She or he uses techniques, treatments, or interventions that have been shown in the scientific literature to be effective for the problem with which the practitioner is faced.

How is such a basis of knowledge regarding treatment efficacy developed? Researchers validate a given treatment for a certain problem or disorder by testing that treatment with individuals who have such a problem. These studies are termed *validation studies*. They verify the treatment as effective (or not) with the designated problem and/or disorder. While it is not the intent of this text to detail the research methodology of validation studies, two important aspects are of relevance to this discussion.

First, researchers conducting these validation studies try to ensure that the subjects participating in the study are representative of those who will be recipients of the treatment if it is found to be successful. For example, if researchers are interested in assessing the efficacy of a certain medication for migraine headaches, the subjects for the study should not be college seniors who get headaches after they drink too much. Rather, it should be subjects who have a documented history of migraines.

The studies that form the evidence base of the classroom management plans contained in this textbook were conducted in special and general education classes across many research sites. Further, the subjects for applied behavior analysis studies typically were students (and/or entire classes) whose teachers were having extreme difficulty in managing their disruptive behavior (Kohler et al., 1995; Lloyd, Eberhardt, & Drake, 1996; Reynolds & Bailey, 1997). These subjects often had levels of problem behavior that were far in excess of "typical" students. Contrast this with classroom management systems that may work for well-behaved children but that can be dismal failures with children who desperately need effective plans.

A second aspect of validation studies is their ability to demonstrate a cause-and-effect relationship between treatment and change in student behavior. Studies that correlate teacher behavior with student behavior *do not* allow for a cause-and-effect analysis. Simply studying what effective teachers do and/or what ineffective teachers do in the classroom does not meet the criteria of a validation study. The validation study must actively manipulate the treatment or management procedure. The treatment condition (often called the experimental condition) is compared with the absence of the treatment condition (or something other than the treatment is being conducted). The latter condition is often referred to as the control condition. The use of an adequate control condition allows the research investigator to unambiguously conclude that the desirable results from the experimental group are not the result of other factors tangential to the treatment procedures.

Much of the validation research conducted in the field of applied behavior analysis has demonstrated, by introducing a control condition, that the change in the children's behavior was a result of the treatment procedure(s) and not some other factor. By exposing the subjects of these studies to both the treatment and control conditions in an alternate fashion, the efficacy of the treatment to alter each subject's behavior in the desired direction can be assessed in a causal manner (Ayllon & Roberts, 1974; Cipani & McLaughlin, 1983; Kern et al., 1995). For further information on cause-and-effect research methodology, refer to other sources (Alberto & Troutman, 2006, pp. 117–167; Bailey & Burch, 2002).

When a series of validation studies verifies similar effectiveness of the proposed treatment with subjects who are representative of the target market group, a sound research base for practice has been developed. For example, the efficacy of token economies and behavioral contingencies on child behavior in classrooms has been repeatedly validated over a 4-decade period (Higgins, Williams, & McLaughlin, 2001; Inkster & McLaughlin, 1993; Kazdin & Bootzin, 1972; McGinnis, Friman, & Carlyon, 1999; O'Leary & Becker, 1967; O'Leary et al., 1969; Pfiffner & O'Leary, 1987; Pfiffner, Rosen, & O'Leary, 1985; Swain & McLaughlin, 1998). Treatment protocols that are developed, inculcating the treatment procedures, are said to be evidence based. *Classroom Management for All Teachers* is like a treatment manual for teachers. It provides a variety of behavioral management systems for classroom use that have empirical support, that is, evidence-based procedures.

THE IMPERATIVE FOR EVIDENCE-BASED PRACTICE

In many fields, to not engage in evidence-based practice is not only professionally unacceptable but also possibly disastrous. Consider the following example. Alzheimer's disease is a debilitating and degenerative disease that is drawing increased attention from pharmaceutical companies. The Food and Drug Administration (FDA) sets up stringent testing requirements before allowing a company to sell a product (treatment) to the American market. This lengthy process provides us, the consuming public, with relative assurances. By the time the medication reaches the market as a prescription, its potential effects and side effects have usually been established. It is the hope of many that in the not too distant future a medication regimen that has an effect on this debilitating disease may be developed. However, the marketing of any drug must be preceded by clinical research data that provide convincing evidence that the drug acts in the manner to which it purports.

What would be the effect on the consumer if the FDA did not impose a scientific or empirical basis for such treatments? Suppose the FDA merely required scientists in the area of Alzheimer's treatments to delineate the theoretical model upon which their drug is based. The scientists would write a book showing how the drug should work, based on chemical, neurological, biological, and/or philosophical theory, and present it to the FDA. In this book, they would have many charts and diagrams showing how their drug fits the proposed model, and they would include testimonials from people who estimate that such a drug, based on this model, will treat Alzheimer's symptoms rapidly. Once the theory is regarded as having merit, the FDA would allow the pharmaceutical company to begin development and marketing.

That review and adoption process should sound dangerous to you. Luckily, the American public and the FDA would not stand for that. If that were the model developed by the FDA, we would all feel less safe about following our physician's recommendations. Not only does one not know whether the drug will work on the symptoms of Alzheimer's disease, but what is also unknown is the potential side effects of the drug. Pharmaceutical companies are not allowed to proceed in such a fashion for obvious reasons. In contrast, as a result of controlled studies, drug researchers provide evidence that their drug has a probable benefit for effectively treating the disorder's symptoms. While these researchers are often highly confident of what will happen, they are always cognizant of the fact that it may not be effective for all patients.

What does happen in science-driven medical practice is the adherence to procedures that are evidence based. Physicians prescribe drugs on the basis of clinical research demonstrating the efficacy of the drug. On the whole, many physicians are less amenable to using eye of newt as a treatment for cancer because a television talk show host had a guest who claimed that his whole family was cured when they had such a diet for 2 weeks. Such testimonials do not constitute scientific proof. One cannot verify that the whole family did have cancer, to what levels the cancer had spread, and whether eating eye of newt was actually the causal agent in their supposed improved condition (also unverified).

I believe the same imperative now exists for the use of evidence-based practice in classrooms. Recently, the passage of the No Child Left Behind (NCLB) Act stipulates the preference for evidence-based interventions in academic areas in the classroom (see www.ed.gov.nclb/landing.jhtml). It will not be long before scrutiny is applied to the manner in which student behavior in the classroom is managed. It is already being judged in special education litigation.

A parent's due process right often brings teachers to litigated cases in which their teaching and/or management practice is brought for open scrutiny by the opposing attorney. Consider the following hypothetical situation involving a case in which the parent's attorney has sued the school for frequent suspensions of John Doe, a junior high student in a special day class.

Scenario:	At fair hearing, with both sets of attorneys, the parent of the child, the hearing officer, and the special education director present, with the teacher providing testimony
Opposing attorney:	Mr. Teacher, you have said that John Doe frequently gets up out of his seat and disturbs other children. Is that correct?
Mr. Teacher:	Yes. Despite my best efforts as a credentialed teacher, John consistently violates the class rule to stay in his seat unless recognized by me. Once out of his seat, he begins to bother several other students. When he does not desist, I have him sent to the principal's office.
Opposing attorney:	And what usually happens there?
Mr. Teacher:	More often than not, he begins to become oppositional to the guidance counselor and the vice principal, Ms. Principal. When Ms. Principal deems he is out of control, she is forced to suspend him.
Opposing attorney:	Mr. Teacher, what management plan do you have that addresses John's out-of-seat behavior and/or his disturbing other students?
Mr. Teacher:	I have tried everything. I have tried talking to him nicely and quietly as was suggested in some text I read.
Opposing attorney:	I would like to get clarification on this point. This technique of talking nicely and quietly—is there evidence-based research literature on this? In other words, Mr. Teacher, are there studies that show it is effective with children like John Doe, who are in special day classes and have problems staying in their seat?
Mr. Teacher:	I was told by my university professors that the author of this book is a highly paid consultant whose theories are followed by many.
Opposing attorney:	Sir, that is not what I am asking. Neither I nor the law is interested in the size of this individual author's bank account. What I am asking is whether those theories actually have research to demonstrate they work with children like John.
Mr. Teacher:	I am not sure.
Opposing attorney:	So let me reiterate. You stated that you are not sure that your practice has any empirical foundation. Yet you continually suspend John for his behavior, with such suspension probably due to the use of an unfounded, ineffective behavioral management plan. Let me ask a related question. Do you have a copy of the functional behavioral assessment and the positive behavioral intervention plan as mandated by IDEA for children who exhibit problems like John?

Mr. Teacher:	I am not sure if either was done.
Opposing attorney:	So I am safe in assuming that you are not following any behavior management plan that would have been specified in either of these "alleged" documents?
Mr. Teacher:	Well. . . .

Anecdotal evidence indicates that suits filed against school districts on behalf of the child and the parents are increasingly questioning the teaching practice as to the empirical evidence base (J. Hartman, personal communication). Using classroom management plans that have an evidence base can provide a reasonable argument in a debate in favor of the existent classroom strategy. Further, the use of such plans can minimize the probability of an evidence-based practicing teacher being put in this position by frequently working, hence reducing the target problem behaviors of individual children. While extensive evidence-based practice in classrooms may not result in no child being left behind, it is my opinion that it would certainly reduce dramatically the number of children who are left behind.

Teachers are faced with minor and major problems every day in their classrooms. Teaching practice that relies on evidence-based approaches can be more effective over the school year in dealing with such problems. Where many books have been written about how to manage student behavior, have the classroom procedures advocated in those books been shown to produce the desired changes? When they do not, what might be the result? I believe the following scenario of a real-life case illustrates my point.

The Case of "He Needs to Cool Off!"

One of my behavioral specialists was assigned a case involving a student in a special day class who was having extreme episodes of aggressive and "agitated" behavior. During the behavioral assessment phase, the specialist sought to identify what might be the reason for such behavior. What he found portrays how unintended consequences occur when an evidence-based approach is not taken. The following is a transcript of the behavioral interview with the teacher.

Teacher:	Robby is just getting worse. We have tried everything to get him to do his work, but he just seems to be more agitated these days. Maybe he needs a different medication.
Behavioral specialist:	How much work is he doing? Is he completing his assignments?
Teacher:	Hardly ever. He just gets so wound up. You know we used to time him out in the corner, but he has just gotten too big for us. He will not go to the corner anymore. On some days, he comes in agitated right from the start.
Behavioral specialist:	What do you do when he is "agitated"? I mean, how do you deal with him, to get him to do his work?
Teacher:	Oh, when he is like that, we cannot get any work out of him. To try would result in getting hit. I am sure you have seen the reports of his aggressive behavior toward the aides and me in the class. We have learned that when he is agitated, he needs to cool off. We send him outside with one of the

	aides from the classroom and tell him to calm down. When he becomes calm, we bring him back inside. Sometimes this takes quite some time. But inevitably, this strategy works.
Behavioral specialist:	(Says "I'll bet" under his breath.) Well, that is interesting. And you reported that he is becoming more frequently agitated, requiring your staff to use this cool-off strategy more regularly?
Teacher:	Yes, that seems to be the pattern. In the beginning of the year, he was only going out once or twice a week. Lately, he goes out several times a day. In some cases, as soon as it is time to engage in his assignment he becomes agitated.

While the cool-off strategy may have seemed like a good idea at the time, note that its use is perpetuating the behaviors comprising agitation. Why would school personnel deem such a strategy best suited for this situation? In fact, there are books and teacher training materials on the market advocating such an approach for children like Robby.

What can be done without incurring Robby's wrath? A three-check task completion system was designed and used for Robby. Robby was given three assignments or tasks to complete that were within his range of capability. For each task he completed successfully, he was given a check. When he earned three checks, he received reinforcement. Guess what the reinforcer was? Time outside. We used the very event Robby was getting when he behaved in an undesirable manner previously.

What were the results of our intervention? No more aggressive behavior, and Robby's agitated behavior was reduced to zero or near-zero. It is important to note that agitated behavior no longer resulted in his being told to go outside and cool off, on the rare occasion it did happen. Robby simply learned that the best way to go outside, with "this new sheriff in town," was to complete his tasks. Congratulations to the school staff for changing their practice and making a huge difference in Robby's life!

RESEARCH PROOF: BUILDING A BETTER MOUSETRAP (PARDON THE PUN)

How many teachers would report that getting their students to attend during oral presentation of material is a mildly to severely difficult task? The phenomenon is so well known that many television sitcoms, movies, and commercials depict students in class snoozing, cutting up, and daydreaming while the teacher lectures. Obviously, many educators want to get students to actively listen to the presentation and respond to teacher questions. If a teacher could get more children to actively attend and respond to teacher questions, then the results would be a greater understanding (and learning) of the presented material.

The traditional method is to ask the class a question and then call on a student to respond to it. Obviously, only one student can answer with this format. Does that mean that the other students are just as attentive as the student who is called upon? Rather, isn't it usually the case that the students most adept with the content are the ones called on frequently to answer questions? The students who need the most practice are the ones who get called on the least, as they learn to exhibit a variety of behaviors that escape the situation when called on, for example, "Uh, ah, I don't know!" With practice, these students acquire even greater skill at avoiding the teacher's questions by acting disinterested, unknowing, and sometimes annoyed that an adult might even consider calling on them.

Is there a more effective and efficient manner of getting many (if not all) students attending during teacher presentations? A technique that has been empirically demonstrated to increase skill acquisition while reducing disruptive behavior would allow teachers to be more assured that their practice is producing a desired result.

Researchers at Ohio State University conducted a study during a social studies period in a regular fourth-grade class with 20 students (Narayan, Heward, Gardner, Courson, & Omness, 1990). They compared the traditional questioning procedure involving the hand-raising (HR) technique versus a unison format termed *response cards* (RC). After every social studies class, a 10-item test was presented to all students covering the material presented during that class as a measure of student learning.

The RC procedure involved presenting questions to the students in the same manner as the hand-raising technique, except that each student would respond to each question using his or her response board. They were supplied with a dry erase board and a dry erase pen (see chapter 11 on Response Cards). The teacher would present the question, for example, "The capital of France is . . . ?" The teacher would then signal the students to write their answer on the dry erase board by saying, "Write." She would count to five and then signal for the students to show their answers to her by saying, "Hold up your board." She then scans the class for each student's answer. If most of the students were correct, she would provide feedback, for example, "I see that most of you wrote 'Paris,' which is the correct answer." If no student answered the question correctly, she would give them the answer. On some days, the RC condition was in effect for the social studies class. On other days, the HR condition was in effect (students did not have access to the dry erase boards during those days).

The results of the research revealed striking differences. During the HR condition for 6 target students, the number of opportunities to respond to a question ranged from 0 to 3 times per class period. During the RC condition, the number of opportunities ranged from 8 to 25 for all 6 students. The total number of responses across all 6 students across the entire study is even more pronounced. During the HR condition, the total number of opportunities to respond to a teacher question was 79, and 1,326 during RC (that's a lot of practice). These contrasting results between HR and RC conditions produced changes in test grades on the 10-item tests, in the following manner (mean number correct over the *entire class*, out of 10 items):

	Mean Correct Test Score
HR 1	7.3
RC 1	*8.2*
HR 2	6.5
RC 2	*7.8*

Also, 19 of the 20 students expressed a preference for the RC technique over the HR procedure. It was anecdotally related to the researchers that

5 to 6 students during HR class periods would stop raising their hands after repeatedly raising their hands to be recognized and not being called on. Furthermore, these same students would often put their heads on the table (and subsequently not participate).

The previous study ends speculation. Is the new alternative to hand raising a more effective technique? Yes, with respect to the number of students who respond to teacher questions and the skill acquisition on 10-item tests. Since this initial study, there have been other studies replicating these results by finding significant changes in student behavior (Armendariz & Umbreit, 1999; Christie & Schuster, 2003; Gardner, Heward, & Grossi, 1994).

WHO NEEDS EVIDENCE-BASED PROCEDURES?

Who needs an evidence-based approach to classroom management? As the title of my book implies, I believe it is all teachers. All teachers come in contact with students who are not performing to adequate levels. Some teachers have one particular student who exhibits severe behavior problems. Their behavior often poses serious problems to the safety and welfare of others, as well as themselves, not discounting the disruption to the learning environment. Other teachers have classes that have frequent disruptions, occurring from several to many students. In other classrooms, no significant disruptions are usually evidenced, but the students' daily performance is less than what it could or should be. All three of these challenging circumstances beg for an approach that has a solid foundation of scientific evidence.

Teacher Challenge 1: Dealing with Extremely Aggressive and Disruptive Students

Suppose you are a sixth-grade teacher. For the most part, your 6 years at that grade level have been good. While you indicate that the majority of the students in your class are "well behaved," your life has not been without headaches. In particular, you remember a year when a particular student created many problems for you; both in the discipline of the class, safety of other children, and your ability to teach. While you certainly have had your share of students who were disruptive from time to time, this particular student tested your very fiber as a professional. That year, incidents occurred with such regularity that you questioned your decision as a former undergraduate to enter the teacher training program.

You have been thinking about that prior student because this year seems like a déjà vu experience. You have a student in your class who has been suspended three times already in this school year, and it is only November! In the first incident, he was suspended for fighting with a fellow classmate during lunch recess, in which the other student had to receive stitches for a laceration caused by his fall during the fight. A second incident involved this student's use of verbal profanity directed toward you, the teacher. All you did was insist that he sit back in his seat and not go to his backpack during class. He frequently disrupts your class and fails to complete assignments. You have constantly attempted to "redirect" him, to get him interested in the material, but to no long-term benefit.

Notes

Take my word for it—you are not alone in this reflection of professional teaching as a career. The majority of the teachers leaving the field in the first several years state that their reason for leaving is caused by the lack of discipline in their classroom. Can any teacher handle this student, let alone get him to profit from instruction? Is there research demonstrating such behavior can be changed by a teacher's implemented strategies?

Research Proof: Dealing with Juvenile Delinquents. Teachers may face students with such severe challenges. A study was conducted with 5 students, aged 14–18 years of age, who were chronic legal offenders (Harris, Finfrock, Giles, Hart, & Tsosie, 1975). These students were committed to the Southwestern Indian Youth Center by federal, state, or tribal courts for offenses such as theft, burglary, or disorderly conduct.

The rate of assignment completion was low for these 5 students. In comparison to the other students in the program, their average completion rate of assignments, over a week, was 37% (range of 20–40%). In the same time period as this baseline, all other 279 students were completing about 65% of their assignments (mean average). In other words, these 5 students were the lowest performers among all the juvenile offenders in this program. If a system could be effective for them, it certainly could work with students who are more motivated in the first place.

A point system provided 300 points to the student if he finished his assignments for the day. Failure to finish an assignment resulted in a 100-point deduction per assignment. Points were traded for privileges in the residence. With the implementation of the program, the average rate of assignment completion for these 5 students jumped 40%, to a mean of 77% (range of 65–95%). In comparison, the same 279 students during this time period completed an average of 67% of their assignments. Now who's on top?

This study exemplifies the strategies that have been found successful in dealing with children who pose severe management problems. You will face some or many students who are difficult to motivate to engage in their assignments, complete their work, and acquire knowledge and skills. Seeing the child "wake up" one day and become a good or great student because of some revelation or epiphany occurs only in the movies (in clinical terms, they often refer to this as "in-sight"). When a transformation occurs, it is because the teacher (and/or parent) has changed the consequences of appropriate and problematic behavior for that student.

Research Proof: Reinforcement Meets Negative Peer Influence! Can a teacher override the influence of peers? I believe the following study (Lau & Cipani, 1984) addresses that point. I was involved as a behavioral consultant with a program for children with severe problem behaviors in the early 1980s. These children were usually removed from the public school setting as a result of unmanageable behaviors. They were placed in a facility where they lived and went to a school on the facility grounds (just for children with severe behavior disorders). One of the teachers I had worked with mentioned a unique problem to me. She had a small class of young boys and was concerned about the amount of food wasted during lunch. She said the children would often throw away more than half of their food (from her perception, often eating only the dessert and some portion of the other food). This occurred despite the fact the children were able to take as much (or as little) as they desired in a cafeteria-style lunch. You can imagine what foods got dumped in the trash bins.

I decided to conduct a systematic study of the effects of a behavioral contingency on food waste, with the teacher agreeing to participate (Lau & Cipani, 1984). We would use just her class in this study. We implemented a system to start measuring plate waste for each lunch period, so that consequences could be brought to bear. Each child was to select a portion of vegetables and the main dish, at whatever amount he desired (as had previously been the case). However, before he emptied the tray, the student was to show the teacher the plate. If it had food on it, the student did not earn points unless he went back and finished it. The points were to be traded in later for time on preferred activities. If the student finished his food, he earned three points for that effort.

The results were quite dramatic across all of the children. The following chart illustrates the percentage of lunches in which food waste occurred for five students. The second and fourth columns in the table represent the period of time when the teacher used the three-point system for food waste. In the third column, the ability to earn three points for finishing the food on your plate was taken away. The only consequence was that the student still had to show the teacher his plate before dumping it.

Percent Food Waste			
Student	**Consequence**	**No Consequence**	**Consequence**
Jack	20	44	Not present
K. K.	0	20	0
K. M.	20	40	0
Vince	40	56	11
Wally	0	70	20

Under the consequence condition, note that a couple of students don't waste food at all! Additionally, a group consequence for food waste was even more effective than the previous results posted for the consequence condition (not shown in the table but found in the article itself). Look at Vince's data. He went from 56% of lunches having food wasted when the only consequence was probably slight embarrassment to 11% (last column) when he would not earn points when he wasted food. Does somebody want to explain how this shows that reinforcement is an ineffective procedure?

What is more impressive is the context under which these results were obtained. All children at this school had behavior problems that resulted in their being sent to this school instead of a public school. Additionally, these results were obtained despite the fact that food waste was being modeled by other students in the lunchroom at the same time. Several classes ate lunch during this period. Only this teacher's class was using a consequence for wasting food. On my observations during the study, it was readily evident that students from other classes were wasting food, throwing large portions of their lunch in the trash bins. How can this be? Don't we hear on a regular basis that children are influenced by their peers and that they pick up bad behaviors when they see their friends do something?

For all the talk about children modeling each other's behavior, the results of this study demonstrate that bad habits can be ameliorated when one uses consequences for that behavior. It was not possible to set up a system for all children in the lunchroom at that time to not waste food. Nor

Notes

did the other teachers appear to be interested in making food waste an issue. However, in spite of the fact that there was negative modeling of food waste, the students in this study wanted to earn points more than imitate their peers. Can consequences for behavior override negative peer influences with students diagnosed with severe behavior disorders? Examine this study and consider that possibility.

Teacher Challenge 2: Daily Encounters with Disruptive Behavior

You might feel that your classroom does not need evidence-based approaches because you do not have anyone who has severe behavioral problems. I have heard many teachers comment, "I do not need behavioral programs. My students are not that bad!" The implication is that one would consider using behavioral plans only for students who are severely disruptive and that the technology does not apply for problems of a lesser nature. Such a conclusion is far from accurate!

Many teachers do face disruptive behavior on a daily basis from any of a select group of students. In many classes, a teacher may have 40–70% of the students do their work, respond to instructions, and perform their daily assignments. However, there may also exist a cadre of students who do not do their work, instead choosing to entertain the rest of the class with their antics. Can evidence-based classroom management strategies be of use in these classrooms? Read the following research studies and be the judge.

Research Proof: What Teachers Do Makes a Difference! Many teachers are plagued daily with a problem referred to as "talking out." In my consultation work, I have termed it "blurting out." Such a behavior involves the student blurting out an answer or statement during teacher instruction and questions to class. What many teachers require is that a student raise his or her hand when they wish to speak, then be recognized, and then speak. Such is authorized talking. Blurting out is not authorized and, if prevalent, can wreak havoc on the learning climate.

Researchers at the University of Kansas examined the effectiveness of behavioral contingencies on frequency of talk outs in a class of 27 second graders (Hall et al., 1971). The school served an urban poverty area. The teacher reported that she considered the class a good class but that talking without the teacher's permission was causing quite a discipline problem. Addressing this behavior involved a considerable amount of class time for her to restore order.

After collecting a baseline on the number of talk outs during 1-hour observation sessions (range of 15–23), the following behavioral plan was carried out by the teacher. Children who raised their hand were praised and called upon. Children who blurted out were ignored, and such behavior was tallied. If the class went below 7 incidents of talk outs during this period, the class could choose a favorite activity/game for that day. What effect did this intervention have? After the first 2 days, the rate of talk outs dropped to 6 or fewer for the next 4 weeks (see the Disruptive Incident Barometer on p. 68).

Not bad, but could it stand improvement? Six or fewer is great, but zero is best. Are these students too impulsive to acquire the ability, without medication, to refrain from blurting out? The teacher then addressed the talk outs of each student with a new contingency. Each student received a straw each day. When a student talked out, the straw was removed. They were told that at the end of the week, they would get a surprise for the number of straws they had in their possession. During a week of implementation, three of the five sessions resulted in no talk outs at all (one occurrence for each of the other days). The difference in the class must have been dramatic.

Note that the change in the manner in which the teacher manages the classroom (i.e., student behavior) results in the change in the student behavior. In other words, behavioral plans empower the teacher to change student behavior for the better. But what if the teacher stops providing praise for hand raising, discontinues the straws, and also starts calling on people who blurt out? You guessed it. Chaos returns rapidly. What a teacher does is a major factor in child behavior. Using contingencies in a behavioral plan produces desirable results. Teaching and managing on the fly—well, you be the judge.

Research Proof: This Stuff Works?—Just Ask a P.E. Teacher in Tallahassee. We have all been in physical education classes as children and probably remember some classes that were in a state of daily chaos. The P.E. teacher's job in managing children is complicated by the inherent fact that physical education class often takes place outside.

Such was the case in a Tallahassee elementary school in the late 1980s (not that only P.E. teachers in Tallahassee have these problems). A P.E. teacher at this elementary school had problems managing two classes in particular. Behavioral researchers Alicia White and Dr. Jon Bailey consulted with this P.E. teacher on this particular problem (White & Bailey, 1990).

To get an idea of the severity of the management problem, the rates of 3 reported problem behaviors were collected in a baseline condition (i.e., the conditions that were typically in effect). The rate of these behaviors in 10-minute observations taken over several days was between 130 and 343 (a mean of 219 occurrences).

The behavioral contingency developed by the researchers to address the high rates of disruptive behaviors in the problematic classes was called "sit and watch." The following behaviors were to produce the sit and watch consequence: (a) failure to comply with teacher request by initiating movement within 5 seconds of instruction, (b) hitting others, and (c) throwing things at others. Contingent on the occurrence of any of the previous behaviors, the child was instructed to take a timer and go to an area away from the activity and sit and watch for 3 minutes. Additional consequences were added to the sit and watch procedure for the first class as an additional means of decreasing such behaviors. If the child went to sit and watch once during the period, she or he would lose daily computer time. If they went to sit and watch more than once during the same period, they also lost a free play period once every 2 weeks. If they engaged in disruptive behavior during sit and watch, they lost free play that day. Finally, if someone talked to a child in sit and watch, they themselves got to experience it.

How did this specific behavioral contingency affect the rate of disruptive behavior relative to the rating system? The mean rate of disruptive behaviors for the first class was 4.6 over the period of the study. The mean rate for the second class was 3.7. What a difference a behavioral contingency can make! Would you say that is a big difference, down from

200 occurrences, in the same time period? Now, that is a P.E. class that is manageable. Who says that behavioral contingencies don't work, and what studies would they be looking at?

Teacher Challenge 3: Unmotivated Students

It would be great if all students came motivated to learn, but it is as sure as the sun rises that many of your students will not perform to their potential day in and day out. An extensive history of studies validates the systems in this book, as the following research studies exemplify.

Research Proof: When Students Study and Attend, They Learn Faster. The beeper system is a technique taught in this book for increasing on-task behavior. One could speculate that increasing on-task behavior would automatically result in an increased acquisition of skills. Such would remain a debatable issue in the absence of validation studies conducted to determine whether such happens. Several researchers (Henderson, Jenson, Erken, Davidsmeyer, & Lampe, 1986) assessed the effectiveness of increasing on-task behavior on student achievement.

To collect the data needed to make this comparison, they collected each student's daily rate of on-task behavior and work completion. Additionally, pretest measures of achievement in math and reading content areas were collected. Once these baseline data were collected on all nine students participating in this validation study, the teacher was trained on the beeper system (see chapter 8). The students were divided into groups of three. During the beep, which occurred at variable intervals, if all three students in the group were on task, the entire group was given points. If one student in the group was not on task at that time, no one in the group received points.

As expected, all the students improved their rate of on-task behavior and work completion. However, what was astounding was the results in achievement. Each student was again administered math and reading achievement tests subsequent to the beeper system being deployed for a period of time. Gain scores were computed for each student by comparing their current grade equivalent score against the previous grade equivalent score. The average grade equivalent gain score for all 9 students was .54 in reading and .77 in math. That is, students averaged about an 80% gain in grade achievement scores over the course of the beeper system.

To highlight the significance of these findings, be reminded that these students had been placed in the resource program because their rate of skill acquisition was slower than that of the average student. The average student in the same time period would have gained .25 grade equivalents in both content areas. What does this mean? For these students—who previously would have not probably achieved even .25 of a gain—they doubled the average gain in reading and tripled the average gain in math. Getting students to do their work reliably will affect how much they learn. Proof positive!

This study verifies what many teachers will tell you: If students engage in their assignments, more often than not they will learn more. When they do not engage in the assignments frequently, they learn less. Now you have a verified procedure for accomplishing that task (see the Beeper System and Task Engagement Program in chapters 8 and 9).

Research Proof: To Stop Disruption, Reinforce Accurate Completion! Does reinforcing accurate completion of class work affect the rate of disruptive behaviors in a fifth-grade class? In a study conducted in Georgia, 5 students whose behavior was ranked as the most disruptive by 2 teachers were selected for study (Ayllon & Roberts, 1974). Prior to behavioral contingency management, the rates of percentage correct on reading assignments and disruptive behavior were taken. This baseline data collection revealed that the percentage correct was between 40% and 50% (an F in anyone's grading system). The rate of disruptive behavior was concurrently high (also about 40–50% of the time). If you are not doing your work, you have to find something to occupy your time with, right?

These researchers addressed the problem in the following fashion. If a child scored 80–99% correct on an assignment, she or he got 2 points; if 100% were correct, she or he got 5 points. Points were traded in for tangible rewards. Would points affect accuracy and disruptive behavior?

When reading and accurate completion produced points, effects to accuracy occurred (no surprise). Additionally, the rate of disruptive behavior went down (surprise, surprise). The final 6 days of the study, where the point system was in effect, produced the following results: Assignment accuracy averaged 85% and disruptive behavior averaged 5%. You see, when students study, they have less time to disturb the environment.

PUNISHED BY REWARDS? I DON'T THINK SO!

Given the previous empirical evidence for using behaviorally based classroom management approaches, why would anyone object to an evidence-based approach? I am often asked the following by many school personnel who attend my workshops: "If these behavioral management systems work so well, how come they are not used that often?" The answer to that question is: Misinformation.

Many future educators are told that the use of contrived external reinforcement to motivate students to perform better, attend for longer periods of time, exhibit disruptive and/or undesirable behaviors less, and complete assignments more is detrimental (Kohn, 1993). In some cases, the following rationale is provided in support of the detrimental argument. "It is not right for students to get rewarded for doing their work. They should do it because it is good for them."

According to that logic, one should not need special diets, programs, or incentives to lose weight, exercise more, or stop smoking, drinking, speeding on the highways, leaving work early, being inaccurate on their tax returns, having unprotected sex, and so forth. One should simply correct those deficits because it is good for you in the long term. Apparently, that is not the case because cottage industries that develop programs, products, and books on such topics have become large enough to be publicly traded companies. If police stopped fining drivers for exceeding the speed limit, what would you predict the effect on speeding would be?

While such logic is often the prevailing reason given for ignoring the applied behavior management literature, research studies have attempted to empirically address the issue (Deci, 1971). The line of this research attempts to determine whether the use of reinforcement for engaging in some task results in less interest in engaging in the same task when no contingent tangible reinforcement is provided. In other words, if a teacher uses the plans delineated in this book, that is, points for staying on task, she or he is making it likely that the child will not want to do the task when points are removed.[2] The research question posed is the following: Do you remove the inherent intrinsic motivation of the student to perform the assignments when reinforcement is withdrawn. Of course, for some students who are starting out with minimal intrinsic motivation to do class assignments, the question seems moot.

The classic experiment initially providing fuel to this argument was performed in a university setting with students in an introductory psychology class who were required to participate in an experiment (this requirement is probably familiar to many of you).[3] Of course, these subjects are not students in elementary or secondary schools exhibiting problem behavior. Contrast this with the research proofs cited previously, where the particular study was conducted in elementary and secondary schools with students who had either behavior and/or academic problems. This huge validity problem in the selection of the study sample, relevant to teachers who work with students with learning and behavioral difficulties in everyday schools makes the generality of the results questionable.

The initial study instituted a research design methodology that involved 2 groups, each with 12 undergraduate members (Deci, 1971). One group was the experimental group (group receiving monetary incentive); the other was the control group (group not receiving monetary incentive). A puzzle task, involving matching configurations to samples of illustrated configurations, was used. All subjects were brought into the experimental room, where the puzzle material was present, as well as several magazines that would be of interest to college students, such as *New Yorker*, *Time*, and *Playboy*. The test situation involved 8 minutes (480 seconds) when the experimenter left the room and the subject was free to work on the puzzle task, do nothing, or read the magazines.

The measure of motivation is the number of seconds spent working on the puzzle task during the 8-minute period, during which the experimenter left the room (but recorded the data via a one-way mirror). The more time spent working on the puzzle, the more the researchers assumed the subject was intrinsically motivated to do the task. The test of the intrinsic hypothesis involved 3 sessions. In the first session, both groups were given the same instructions before the experimenter left the room. "You can work on whatever you want, I need to go do something," the experimenter might say. The amount of time each subject spent on the puzzle task was recorded with a stopwatch. The maximum possible was 480 seconds.

In the second session, the control group was given the same instructions and procedures as before, that is, you are free to choose what you want to do. The experimental subjects were told that they would be given one dollar for each puzzle they correctly matched to the sample provided

---

[2] A question to consider: If you were able to take a 6-year-old child who ran around the room, spending only 10% of the class time actually doing work, and got him to do his work 80–90% of the time, would you want to stop doing whatever was creating that wonderful scenario?

[3] Many psychology theories are based on studies using college students. I believe a best-selling book might be *Everything We Want to Know About Mental Health and Human Behavior We Learned from Studying College Sophomores Who Were Getting Lab Credit.*

(remember, a couple of dollars could buy a tank of gas back then). In the third session, both groups were again equated.

The use of monetary reinforcement for the experimental group was a test of the intrinsic motivation decrement hypothesis. If such a hypothesis is true, the third session would show lower levels of working on the puzzle task for the experimental group when compared to the first session. The following data were obtained for both groups, reporting the average number of seconds the 12 subjects in each group worked on the puzzle task.

Mean Number of Seconds Spent on Puzzle Task			
Group	Session 1	Session 2	Session 3
Experimental	248	314	199
Control	214	206	242

Note that the difference between the first and third session in the experimental group is one of less puzzle time. Hence, the author (and many others) concluded that reinforcement reduces intrinsic motivation. The control group fluctuates between higher performance (e.g., 242 seconds) and lower performance (206 seconds).[4]

While the control group's fluctuations escaped the author's attention (e.g., "Why were they slacking off in the first and second sessions?"), something even more striking was not pointed out in the author's interpretation of these data. What happened to the performance of the experimental group when monetary reinforcement was provided (i.e., second session data)? It shot up; that is, those subjects worked more on the task than they had in the first session, seemingly restraining themselves from spending a lot of time looking at entertaining magazines. Note that the performance of the control group in any of the 3 sessions does not even come close to 314 seconds. If you are a teacher, you want to increase the amount of time students spend doing some task, and you know that the effect of a unique task will wear off, what do you want to do? What do the data say is the best way to increase the on-task level of students? Reinforcement.

However, another experiment in the same article (Deci, 1971) provides an even greater rationale for using reinforcement procedures. This experiment replicated the procedures used in the first study with another 24 "volunteers." Except in this case, verbal approval was given (e.g., "That is very good.") instead of money. The data from the control group present an even more compelling reason for teachers to deploy reinforcement to maximize students' motivation.

Mean Number of Seconds Spent on Puzzle Task			
Group	Session 1	Session 2	Session 3
Experimental	134	147	129
Control	247	146	65

---

[4] It is often the case that when you fail to reinforce behavior and performance, variability becomes more marked. Keep this variability in mind for the next set of data when looking at the control group.

Again the experimental group shows a difference between first and third sessions, in the form of a decrement in puzzle time (a 5-second difference across all subjects). However, this experimental group did not have that huge jump in performance like the subjects in the first study. The effects of verbal reinforcement for these 12 subjects were not as dramatic as monetary reinforcement for the subjects in the earlier study (imagine that!).

An even more alarming finding involved the control group in this experiment. In the first session, these subjects apparently had "a lot" of intrinsic motivation to engage in the puzzle task (mean of 247 seconds). But look at the mean number of seconds in the next 2 sessions, that is, 146 and 65 seconds respectively. Where is their intrinsic motivation in Sessions 2 and 3? Have teachers seen this type of student performance in their classrooms—great for a while and then performance takes a nosedive?.

In regard to this huge decrement in the control group, the author (Deci, 1971) wrote, "It is difficult to account for this." Well, it isn't difficult to account for this. Without reinforcement, you get markedly less performance over time (i.e., students get bored with the previously intriguing task). In Sessions 2 and 3, intrinsic motivation was not at optimal levels for the control group. If you were the teacher of the control group, should you just wait for those days when their intrinsic motivation is optimal? When one fails to use the power of reinforcement, one hopes that the students woke up on the right side of the bed and are ready to work on a given day.

The moral of this story: You should not just rely on intrinsic motivation when you need students attending and performing at consistent levels, day in and day out. When you need to motivate students to perform week after week and to prevent boredom, use reinforcement! Plain and simple. You need to acquire the skills in this book to be maximally effective with many (if not all) students in your class.

WANTED: INTRINSICALLY MOTIVATED STUDENTS

Any person who teaches as a profession would obviously prefer that students come to class "intrinsically motivated." We would all like to have students who engage in study simply with a verbal directive to do so, who work hard to pass or excel at the tests, and listen to our every word with utter delight. That's the goal.

Wanting students to engage in study behavior without any contrived reinforcement other than grades is a desirable end. But do all students come to school intrinsically motivated? What can a teacher do when faced with a number of students who do not care to work on the assignments, do well on tests, or study when needed? It is important to not confuse the goal (self-motivated students) with how it can be achieved in students who do not yet possess the love of learning. However, I believe there is something teachers can do to develop such a student where one does not exist. Put simply: Develop competence.

Your ultimate goal is to develop students who are competent in learning. This is initially demonstrated by their performance on daily assignments and tests. Consider this a short-term goal that leads eventually to the long-term goal. What you do in class should be directed toward achieving the short-term goal, and the long-term goal will follow. When students become competent in the current instructional content, you will have less of a need to contrive reinforcement.

Is it not the case, generally speaking, that the students who are doing well and answer all the teacher's questions are the ones no one has to motivate? In contrast, the students who are doing poorly usually seem to be the ones that school personnel label as not motivated. Can it be that competence breeds the will to succeed? Succeeding at a task makes one more willing to try similar, more challenging tasks.

If incompetence with academic material breeds problem behavior (Weeks & Gaylord-Ross, 1981), what needs to be done? When students are taught well and they rehearse the skills many times, competence is more likely to follow. With competence arriving, behavior problems are departing.

The Case of Developing Competence Is the Key!

Vivian was a 6-year-old girl headed in the wrong direction. She was presenting difficulty to the people who cared for her, both at home and school. In the foster home where she resided, she regularly engaged in oppositional and defiant behavior. She was removed from a foster family for such behaviors prior to my involvement and was headed toward the same result in her current home. The current foster parents had given a 7-day notice for social services to remove her if the situation did not get better. The problems reported in the home environment were failure to follow house rules, being disrespectful toward foster parents, tantrums, and noncompliance to adult requests. Reports attributed this inability to get along with adults as a function of nonexistent discipline from her biological parent (father), who raised her until she was removed from his "care."

I immediately addressed such problems with behavioral interventions. To everyone's good fortune, the behavioral plans worked extremely well in the home environment and the notice to move her was rescinded. However, the problems reported during the prior school placement resurfaced during her attendance at summer school. Vivian was required to go to summer school because she was far below grade level in reading and math and would not be promoted without attending summer school to make up the difference. Reports from the previous teacher indicated that she would often verbally refuse to do an assignment. "I can't do that" and "I won't do that" were common cries. Such behaviors resulted in the teacher either not pressing her at that point (which, of course, was to Vivian's delight) or pressing her to try. At that point, Vivian would throw a tantrum, and not much work would get done in either case. The reports from the previous teacher indicated that verbal refusal in the morning meant no work was going to be done that day. It was no wonder that she was way behind. In order to learn, you have to engage in the assignments and attend to the teacher when she is presenting. There are many kids like Vivian who fail to learn because they do not have the skill of "independent" study and engage in all other kinds of interfering behaviors, usually bothering others, which was certainly the case here as well.

The summer school teacher reported the same phenomenon immediately, and Vivian's foster parent and I went into action. We targeted this verbal refusal the first week of school with a home-based reinforcement plan. Vivian was told that each day she refused to do her work, the teacher would send a note home to her foster mother and call. If the call was made, indicating refusal to perform an assignment, she went to bed 1 hour early that night (this is what worked so well with her home compliance problems). Additionally, outside privileges with the neighborhood kids were revoked for that day. On days when she engaged in her assignments, all privileges were reinstated and her foster mother provided heavy doses of praise. The program worked like a charm. In roughly a 5-week period, the teacher had to report opposition only once. In addition to the removal of her opposition to assignments, a nice benefit occurred: Vivian actually began to learn how to read. Her improvement in academics was rated as "much" by the summer school teacher.

When September came, the same plan was put into effect for verbal opposition for her new first-grade teacher. Just as before, it worked well. However, other problems not addressed by this plan were surfacing. Vivian lived with her foster parent as an only child in the house. This makes contact and conversation with peers a desirable activity. While she was no longer opposing school work, she tended to be quite a "talk show host" during instruction. Such frequent behavior on her part was getting her in trouble.

The teacher had attempted to gain control over unauthorized conversations as well as any other general unacceptable behaviors by using lunch recess as a consequence. This plan was disastrous. Vivian was spending every recess period on the "wall." There was no noted improvement in her behavior. I met with the teacher and indicated that the consequence, the loss of recess, was probably a sufficient consequence to use. However, making the target behavior, any "misbehavior," would always result in Vivian losing recess. After a while she would just give up trying to earn recess (learned helplessness). After collecting baseline data on the frequency of blurting out, we collectively agreed on the following plan for blurting out.

1. State the rule about blurting out to Vivian at the beginning of each day and present her with a card.

2. No warnings were subsequently given.

3. Contingent on each occurrence, Vivian lost her card, which resulted in removal from the group for a 3-minute period (she took her work with her, just changed her seating assignment).

4. If the card was removed more than seven times in a day (gives you an idea of how often in the baseline she was blurting out), she lost recess the next day and a call home occurred.

5. If she did not lose the card at all, she got a 1-minute public conversation time at the end of the day.

At the end of the 2 weeks, Vivian was not losing recess. The teacher reported that she usually did not lose her card more than 3 times in a given day. Only once did she lose recess. This represents a huge difference in unauthorized talking. In the following 2 months, inappropriate behavior had been added as an additional requirement, the removal from the group had been withdrawn, and the standard was now 3 or under for both sets of behaviors. I ended my involvement at this point and told the teacher and parent to continue with the program.

For the critics who claim that behavior modification produces only short-term effects, Vivian's teacher and foster parents want to take issue. At the end of the school year, of her own volition, Vivian's mother called me to report that Vivian had done great and that her teacher was so pleased with her. Her foster parent reported that she could not remember the last time she lost home privileges. It is important to note that effective contingencies work so well in the long run that they rarely have to be applied. One might say the child is intrinsically motivated to do well!

Her report card revealed the following during the third-trimester grading period (S = satisfactory, O = outstanding):

Vivian's Report Card		
Subject	**Progress**	**Effort**
Oral/Language	O	O
Reading	O	O
Spelling	O	O
Math	S	S

These results are impressive. Remember, this was a girl who couldn't read prior to summer school. Note that she received an outstanding in reading, spelling, and oral language.

At the beginning of the year, as a result of her behavior in kindergarten, Vivian was a girl at risk for failing at an early age in the educational system. She is like many other kids who drop into a downward spiral right from the beginning. Except, in this case, a parent and teacher turned the tide. They not only got Vivian to do her work, but developed a competent learner. What would Vivian have received on this report card if her verbal refusal had not been addressed successfully? One can only guess.

DEVELOPING COMPETENT LEARNERS: THE CASE FOR INTRINSIC MOTIVATION

The behavioral plans in this book provide a vehicle for students to become competent learners. These plans directly reduce behaviors that will interfere with the student's ability to learn, as well as increase behaviors that involve active engagement in the instruction, whether that be attending to lectures/presentations or independent study.

However, effective management strategies *cannot override poor instruction*. In order for students to acquire skills, the manner in which you teach makes a big difference. If your method of instruction leaves many students unskilled in the target area(s), a Good Behavior Board Game is not going to rescue the day. The students may be better behaved, but the ultimate reason for their being there is not accomplished: learning skills that will make them productive citizens. These students, in whom competence is not developed, probably will not demonstrate the behaviors indicative of "intrinsic motivation." It is not within the scope of this book to address instructional procedures, but suffice it to say that not all instructional procedures are created equal (or effective).

One plan presented in this book can develop more powerful instructional procedures. Response Cards is both a procedure that accomplishes effective management of behavior and an effective instructional procedure for learning. As a method of teaching it can be very powerful, both for its effect on behavior as well as its ability to have students acquire new skills. Be liberal in its use. If your students spend 90% of the day doing seat work, increase the amount of direct teaching time by using Response Cards in several content areas (refer to chapter 11 for details).

I hope this chapter has taught you that "you can make a difference in a child's school behavior." You don't have to wait for all societal ills to be solved. If you are now sold on the plea to become an evidence-based practitioner, the next two parts of this book address specific plans, drawn from the scientific literature in applied behavior analysis that can be aids to you in the classroom.

PART 2

Plans for Reducing or Eliminating Disruptive and Rule-Violation Behavior

Chapter 2

The Good Behavior Board Game

Chapter 3

Behavioral Contracting

Chapter 4

Individual Disruptive Incident Barometer

Chapter 5

Signal Time-Out for Minor Disruptive Behavior

Chapter 6

Removal Time-Out for Severe Disruptive and Aggressive Behavior

Chapter 7

Positive Compliance Momentum

INTRODUCTION

WHAT IS DISRUPTIVE BEHAVIOR?

Disruptive behavior can take many forms. Minor forms involve the following types of behavior: out-of-seat, unauthorized talking, loud talking, or other behaviors that disrupt the learning environment. In more severe forms, the disruption to the learning environment is substantial and may jeopardize the welfare and safety of the individual child, teacher, or other children. Examples of severe types of disruptive behavior include physical aggression (e.g., hitting or striking another child with an object), property destruction (e.g., grabbing and throwing a book, tearing up paper or books, or hitting the desk or wall with an abrupt and forceful action), and verbally abusive behavior (e.g., profanity, name-calling, scolding, or throwing tantrums).

Classroom rule violations are also categorized as disruptive behaviors. Teachers designate rules that help them provide instruction to students in an organized and effective manner. When rules are not adhered to, the teacher's ability to present effective instruction is proportionally diminished.

The types of rule violations can range from mild to severe. Mild violations include getting out of the seat without permission, unauthorized talking to a peer, chewing gum, and speaking without raising one's hand. Severe violations are the same types of behaviors described earlier under severe disruptive behaviors.

The ramifications of continued disruptive behavior are considerable. Even mild disruptive behaviors or rule violations can affect the learning environment. For example, children who are frequently out of their seats will not be able to complete many seat assignments or attend to the teacher's instructions. As one might imagine, eventually the performance of the children deteriorates if they cannot stay in their seats long enough to learn new material.

Children who continually break class rules disrupt the classroom learning environment. For example, a child who incessantly chatters to another student during in-seat work not only disrupts the learning environment for him and the student he talks to, but also disrupts the environment of other students in the vicinity. Also, the teacher's ability to control the classroom environment is lessened.

DEALING WITH DISRUPTIVE BEHAVIOR

Teachers and other school personnel attempt to deal with disruptive behaviors and rule violations with several common strategies. I call one such strategy *rule reminder*. The teacher restates the rule when a child commits a rule violation. For example, a child may get out of his seat without permission and the teacher may comment, "Johnny, the class rule is that you stay in your seat unless you raise your hand and ask permission to leave your seat." The child may then sit in his seat for a period of time after that reminder. However, eventually he gets out again and the teacher reminds him of the rule. The child returns to his seat. After several more unauthorized excursions out of seat, the teacher abandons this strategy, claiming it is useless for this child.

When restating the rule does not produce student adherence to the rules, teachers often add verbal admonishment or threats as a consequence: "Johnny, you are constantly breaking the rules and getting out of your seat. Please discontinue this or I will be forced to deal with you in a more punitive manner." Once again, when this strategy does not change the child's behavior, it is discontinued, or used only intermittently.

Sometimes, teachers will establish incentives as a strategy to deal with disruptive behavior. While incentives can produce changes in a child's behavior, there are many reasons that they might not work. For example, a teacher may arrange an incentive that can be earned after too long a period of time to be effective (e.g., 2 weeks, 3 weeks, or a month). Some children may need something more immediate. An incentive also probably will not work if the behavior standard set by the teacher is way above the child's ability. The initial behavior standard usually does not take into account the child's current baseline level. Subsequently, the child is unable to earn the incentive during the first few opportunities. Eventually, the child becomes unmotivated to respond to the "possibility" of earning an incentive (not a strong possibility for him).

Finally, for more severe types of disruptive behavior, strategies such as sending the child to the principal's office or suspension or expulsion are used. A child who is repeatedly sent to the principal's office eventually does not find this consequence particularly aversive. It therefore does not deter him from engaging in further disruptive behavior. The same can be said for the suspension/expulsion strategy, which is used when the teacher and principal have tried everything they can think of and nothing has worked.

EFFECTIVE STRATEGIES FOR DISRUPTIVE BEHAVIOR

Teachers dealing with disruptive behavior should initially focus on increasing appropriate behavior. This effort to increase appropriate behavior should be through the use of a management strategy to increase (reinforce) on-task behaviors and assignment completion (see part 3 of this book). Disruptive behavior often can be reduced a significant degree by increasing the child's completion rate of assigned work and on-task behavior (Barrish, Saunders, & Wolf, 1969; Dietz & Repp, 1973; Speltz, Wenters-Shimamaura, & McReynolds, 1982). If on-task and attending behaviors are increased through reinforcement, the child will engage in problem behaviors less often.

The behavioral plans discussed in detail in this section are listed in the following chart. This list also indicates whether the plans can be used as a classwide system, or for individual students, or both.

Six Management Plans for Addressing Disruptive Behavior		
Behavioral Technique	**Classwide**	**Individual**
Good Behavior Board Game	X	
Behavioral Contracting		X
Individual Disruptive Incident Barometer		X
Signal Time-Out	X	X
Removal Time-Out		X
Positive Compliance Momentum	X	

These plans have an empirical track record of ameliorating problem behaviors and increasing appropriate behaviors. However, in some individual cases, an analysis of the problem behavior's environmental function may be required for a long-term solution (Iwata, Dorsey, Slifer, Bauman, & Richman, 1994; Kennedy, Meyer, Knowles, & Shukla, 2000). While these management plans are well grounded in the principles of human behavior, they may not take into account the unique and idiosyncratic functions some problem behaviors may serve in particular classrooms. In those cases, and in keeping with the requirements of the 2004 reauthorization of the 1997 IDEA legislation, a functional behavioral assessment should be conducted. It is not within the scope of this text to fully address the requirements and knowledge base needed for such an assessment. However, I strongly encourage special educators, administrators, and school psychologists to consult sources that address the analysis of behavioral function and functional positive behavioral treatments (see www.geocities.com/voivod00 for material on a functional analysis of behavior model for school settings).

2

The Good Behavior Board Game

BRIEF DESCRIPTION

The Good Behavior Board Game is a mechanism for managing problem disruptive behaviors during independent seatwork and/or lesson presentation for the whole class. This management system is derived from the Good Behavior Game delineated in the second edition of this text (Cipani, 2004). The Good Behavior Game is a useful strategy for a group of students or the entire class (Barrish, Saunders, & Wolf, 1969; Carpenter & McKee-Higgins, 1996; Harris & Sherman, 1973; Medland & Stachnik, 1972). The Good Behavior Game has even seen international verification from a study conducted with Sudanese students (Saigh & Umar, 1983). This version presents a management system that covers the entire class as a single group, in the form of a board game. Tracking the class as a single group (in contrast to multiple groups) may be less cumbersome for teachers, particularly with larger classes.

The Good Behavior Board Game involves rewarding good behavior by allowing the class to move their game piece or icon around the game board maze contingent on intervals of good behavior. The game board maze (see Form 2.1) is posted in plain view at the front of the classroom. The objective of the game is for the class (as a team) to progress through the game board maze to the treasure box spots. When the team icon gets to a treasure box spot, a student from the team draws a slip of paper from the treasure box. Each slip has a designated rewarding activity or item written on it (see list of possible rewards for the treasure box in Form 2.2). Everyone in the class gets that selected prize or activity at a teacher-designated time during the day.

The Good Behavior Board Game incorporates good behavior rules that form the basis for playing the game. Good behavior is defined as the absence of violations of specified classroom rules. The teacher specifies and posts the rule violations for seatwork and/or lesson presentation (see Form 2.3) and how long the instructional period will last. The class must meet the behavior goal for each good behavior interval in order to move the class icon one space on the game board. Rules for playing the game should also be posted (Form 2.4).

A good behavior interval, such as 10 minutes, is designated before the start of the instructional period. An oven timer visible to the students is set for that length of time. If the team reaches their good behavior goal for a particular interval, the class icon moves 1 space on the maze. The next interval is then set for another 10 minutes, with the same behavior goal and rules. Each time the class meets the behavior goal in a given interval, the icon moves another space. If the class fails to reach the behavior goal, the class icon does not move. With the end of each interval, the class begins another attempt at reaching the behavior goal for the following interval until the end of the instructional period. In summary, the progress of the class on the board game maze is contingent on their performance during the good behavior intervals.

TERMS

behavior goal the target number of class violations in a good behavior interval that allows the icon to move one space on the game board.

good behavior interval the unvarying interval length established for the class to meet the behavior goal. I suggest 10 minutes for most classes with the exception of younger grades (K–2), which may designate 5-minute intervals.

APPARATUS

- Game Board Mazes (Form 2.1)[1]
- Classroom Rule Violations Chart (Form 2.3)
- Good Behavior Board Game Rules (Form 2.4)
- Rule Violation Chart—Baseline (Form 2.5)
- Rule Violation Chart (Form 2.6)
- Oven Timer
- Treasure Box (any sizable box, e.g., shoe box with a cover, coffee can with a cover; anything large enough for a student to put hand in)
- Slips of paper for writing prizes earned and placing in the treasure box
- List of possible earned activities (Form 2.2)

BASELINE MEASUREMENT

The purpose of the baseline measurement for the Good Behavior Board Game is to enable the teacher to determine a reasonable behavior goal for each good behavior interval. The teacher determines which instructional period(s) the board game will be used. The teacher then counts and records the rule violations for each good behavior interval during the designated time period(s) within each good behavior interval. During the baseline phase, only feedback on each interval is posted on the baseline data sheet. The game board maze is not used at this time. To enhance motivation, the teacher can challenge the class to beat their previous score each day during the baseline. The baseline phase should be at least 9 to 12 days, or until the class has reached a representative level of performance. (See Form 2.5.)

The importance of collecting baseline data prior to implementing the board game cannot be overstressed. In addition to gaining a more accurate assessment of the rate of rule violations across the entire class, the baseline data serves an additional function. The use of baseline data in setting the initial behavior goal can frequently determine the success or failure of the Good Behavior Board Game.

When baseline data are not used in determining the target goal, the criteria for success is often arbitrarily determined. As a hypothetical example, Mr. Vee decides that there should be no instances of rule violations across the entire good behavior interval (10 minutes) for the class to move a space up on the board. Hence the class' capability to achieve the goal may be grossly overestimated. In the first 2 weeks of class, the class gets to only 1 treasure box. With the class continually failing to reach the

[1]For an electronic file of the game maze in color, go to www.geocities.com/voivod00

target goal for the good behavior interval, the program eventually falls into oblivion. Mr. Vee concludes (incorrectly) that his class has too many students who are disruptive for any system to work. Mr. Vee might have been successful if a more reasonable behavior goal had been set, by considering the current baseline rate of his class. While it may take some additional effort on the part of Mr. Vee, it would have been well worth that effort. When the target goal is arbitrarily set without considering baseline data, failure of a potentially successful intervention may occur.

Once the baseline data are collected, the teacher needs to determine a reasonable behavior goal for the class by examining the baseline data across all the days they were collected. For each day calculate the average (mean) number of rule violations across all 10-minute periods.

Rule Violation Chart—Baseline	
Date: April 16 **Instructional Period: Pre-Algebra**	
10-Minute Interval	**Tallies of Rule Violations**
First	+ +
Second	+ + + + + +
Third	+ + + +
Fourth	0
Fifth	+ + + + + + + + + + +
Sixth	+ + + + + + + + + +
Seventh	+ + +
Eighth	+ + + + +
Ninth	+ + + + +

Range of rule violations: 0–11
Average number: about 5

The teacher does this for each day of the baseline. Based on an examination of this data, a reasonable behavior goal is designated (the average across all baseline sessions/days is a good method to use).

PROCEDURES

- Collect baseline data for 9–12 days.
- Inform the students of the rules of the Good Behavior Board Game, the behavior goal, and potential class rewards in the treasure box spots.
- Post all charts in plain view.
- At the beginning of the target class period, set the oven timer for 10 minutes and proceed with the class lesson or seat work.
- Record rule violations as they occur in the respective 10-minute intervals on the posted chart (see sample Rule Violation Chart).
- When the timer goes off, record the total number of violations on the Rule Violation Chart and determine whether the class reached the behavior goal.

- If the class stayed at or under the behavior goal, advance their class icon a spot on the maze; if not, do not move the icon.
- Reset the timer for another 10 minutes.
- Repeat the same steps delineated above for each 10-minute interval, such as a 30-minute instructional period would be 3 intervals of 10 minutes.
- If using the Board Game for a second instructional period, pick up the game where you left off (i.e., leave class icon on game board).

Once the board game is implemented, the tracking form used is the Rule Violation Chart (see following sample). The teacher records each rule violation as done previously, but at the end of the interval, she or he marks whether the class met the behavior goal (and whether to move the icon on the game maze). The sample Rule Violation Chart is filled out for a 90-minute session.

Rule Violation Chart		
Good Behavior Goal: 6 or fewer for the interval **Date: May 4** **Instructional Period: Math Lesson and Seat Work**		
10-Minute Interval	**Tallies of Rule Violations**	**Met Goal?**
First	+ + + +	Yes
Second	+ + +	Yes
Third	0	Yes
Fourth	+ + +	Yes
Fifth	+ + + + + + + +	No
Sixth	+ + +	Yes
Seventh	+ + + + + +	Yes
Eighth	+ + + + + + + + + +	No
Ninth	+ + +	Yes

Number of successful intervals / Total number of intervals: 7/9

The Rule Violation Chart shows that during the math period, nine 10-minute intervals comprised the playing time for the board game. The class (team) met the behavior goal in all but 2 of the intervals, getting to move their game icon 7 spots on the game board maze. In the third interval, the class had no rule violations. The class failed to reach the good behavior goal in only 2 intervals; in the fifth interval (8 rule violations) and in the eighth interval (10 rule violations).

HOW IT WORKS

The Good Behavior Board Game works by providing an achievable behavior goal for the entire class. The standard for good behavior is initially set for a reasonable level of disruptive behaviors or rule violations. As the children get better at controlling their behavior, the behavior goal for the class can be gradually lowered until a desirable level is achieved. Too often, the behavioral goal for an individual or class earning reinforcement is arbitrarily set, without consulting baseline data. This initial standard can be too high, making it improbable that the students will achieve it in the short term. With the failure to achieve the standard and earn reinforcement, the students give up, rendering the behavioral contingency impotent. By using baseline data in determining the initial behavior goal, the teacher can avoid such a result.

Another powerful component of this management system is the public posting of each infraction for each interval. By recording each instance of a rule violation as it occurs, all the students in the class are apprised of their progress toward the behavior goal during each interval. Since the game is composed of multiple intervals throughout the instructional session, the class has multiple opportunities to progress toward the treasure box. Missing the goal for a given interval does not prevent the class from earning a backup reinforcer. Rather, the opportunity to progress on the game board becomes available within a short period of time, such as 10 minutes.

The Good Behavior Board Game uses a group contingency (Pigott & Heggie, 1986; Siagh & Umar, 1983; Speltz et al., 1982). Unlike an individual contingency, the performance of the group determines the group's access to reinforcement. There are certain advantages to the use of a group contingency, such as the removal of peer reinforcement for misbehavior. For many classes in which disruptive behavior is maintained by peer attention and approval, the Good Behavior Board Game can produce a desirable effect where an individual contingency would be ineffective.

ADDITIONAL CONSIDERATIONS

Children Who Are More Disruptive Than Others

It is possible that one or several children in the group might consistently alter the class' ability to achieve the behavior standard. This possibility is lessened significantly by two factors: (1) using the average number of rule violations from the baseline data in setting the behavior goal and (2) the removal of peer attention for misbehavior as a result of the group-oriented contingency. In spite of these two operative factors, it is possible that one child may consistently account for the class missing the behavior goal across a number of intervals. In this case, the teacher might remove this child from the game and consider an individual behavior contract. Once this child's level of disruptive behavior approximates the lower level displayed by the other children in the class, she or he can be included again.

Provide Intermittent Praise for Nondisruptive Behavior

The teacher can intermittently scan the class and praise students who are doing their work and not engaging in disruptive behavior. Although the Good Behavior Board Game requires the teacher to monitor disruptive incidents, it should not exclude the use of praise and attention for appropriate (nondisruptive) behavior.

HYPOTHETICAL EXAMPLE

Use of Classwide Good Behavior Board Game for a Tenth-Grade Math Class

Mrs. Young, a high school math teacher, is concerned about the frequent outbursts in two of her math classes. Such outbursts occur during her lecture while she is demonstrating the procedural requirements for solving problems in algebra or geometry. For example, one day as Mrs. Young was about to demonstrate how to simplify radical expressions, one of the boys shouted out, "Hey, dude, the more radical the better, I always say." While this comment may be great for stand-up comedy, such outbursts often arouse peer attention and distract the class from the lesson. Then the class becomes a "competition" for the best wisecrack. The frequency of such interrupting comments and jokes has definitely increased to the point where it is difficult to finish a lesson for the day. Given state requirements for competence, particularly in algebra for all high school students, Mrs. Young is worried that such a pattern of behavior will affect the amount of material she can cover.

Mrs. Young is convinced that simply asking the students to demonstrate self-control will not be the answer. She knows there is too much interest and attention given to the comedy routine by class members. She will begin the Good Behavior Board Game in the first-period class and will implement it in the fourth-period class several weeks hence. She collects baseline data in the first period for 12 days on the rate of outbursts according to 10-minute intervals. Each time a student makes an unauthorized comment, joke, or statement during her lecture or during independent seat work, she counts it within the respective interval.

After examining the baseline data (which indicated a rate of behavior between 0 and 9 outbursts with a mean of 2 per interval), she designates the behavior goal for the class at 2 or fewer for each 10-minute interval. She gets the game board ready, along with the treasure box. In the treasure box, she places 30 slips of paper delineating various reinforcers the class can earn for landing on the treasure box spot. For example, there are slips with 5 or 10 minutes of social conversation time; 5, 10, or 15 minutes of time allotted to do homework in class; 5 or 10 minutes of leisure activity time such as looking at teen magazines with friends; and other such prized activities.

Mrs. Young implements the Good Behavior Board Game during the first period while beginning baseline data collection in the fourth period. She informs the class of the rules of the board game and places the rules on the bulletin board: Do not make comments, outbursts, or statements during lecture or seat work that are unauthorized and unrelated to algebra. Mrs. Young records instances of target behavior (i.e., outbursts) during the respective interval on the data sheet. After each interval, the class icon moves up a square if the class met the behavior goal.

Across the first 2 weeks of the Good Behavior Board Game, the rate of outbursts dropped below 2 or fewer outbursts for over 85% of the intervals. The class has definitely gotten the idea and apparently enjoys earning conversation time and ability to do the homework in class (instead of at home). On the basis of these data, Mrs. Young now selects a new behavior goal—1 or fewer! She also initiates the board game with the fourth-period class. The baseline data proved they needed it as well (range 3–16!). She anticipates similar good results and is considering using the board game for all her classes. Algebra is so much easier to teach when the class is focused on her lecture and not waiting for the next cute comment from the class clowns!

WHAT IF?

- What might Mrs. Young do if one member of her fourth-period class continues to make outbursts?
- What could she do if the logistics of summating data every 10 minutes are proving difficult?
- Do you think the reinforcers in the treasure box should be changed every few weeks? Why or why not?

FORMS

2.1 Good Behavior Board Game Mazes

2.2 List of Possible Earned Activities

2.3 Classroom Rule Violations Chart for seat work and/or lesson presentation: for posting

2.4 Good Behavior Board Game Rules: for posting

2.5 Rule Violation Chart—Baseline: record frequency of target rule violations in the respective 10-minute interval

2.6 Rule Violation Chart: record frequency of target rule violations and whether the class met the behavior goal in the respective 10-minute interval

2.7 Weekly Summary Sheet

FORM 2.1

Good Behavior Board Game Mazes

─── **FORM 2.2** ───

List of Possible Earned Activities

Note to Teacher: Put each activity, such as 3 minutes of silent ball, 5 minutes of silent ball, or 3 minutes of drawing, on a separate slip of paper that is folded so the student cannot see the words when selecting from the treasure box. Make as many slips as you need. Students can spend or save their time on earned activities. In order to make the board game even more powerful as a motivating system, place fewer slips for the bigger prizes (e.g., 10-minute break card) in contrast to the smaller prizes (e.g., 2-minute break card). While there may be only one 10-minute break card in the treasure box, there can be four 2-minute break cards (thus decreasing the odds that the students will frequently select 10-minute break cards). Obviously, these are but a few suggestions. See appendix A for additional ideas on potential reinforcers.

Earned Doodling/Drawing Time

1. 3 minutes of doodling/drawing time

2. 5 minutes of doodling/drawing time

3. 2 minutes of doodling/drawing time

4. 4 minutes of doodling/drawing time

Class Activity

1. 3 minutes of silent ball time (using a beach ball)

2. 5 minutes of silent ball time

3. 2 minutes of silent ball time

4. 4 minutes of silent ball time

The Strongest Link—Academic Game

1. Divide the students into 4–5 teams, trying to equate for ability across teams within the content area selected for the game.

2. Each team is given a dry erase board.

3. Pose questions in the content area (e.g., math, spelling, punctuation, reading) that have a short answer (i.e., no more than 3–4 words).

4. Each team has a designated time on the oven timer to collectively come up with the answer.

5. When the timer goes off, each team shows its answer and the teacher rules as to the correctness of the written response.

6. Each team that answers the question correctly gets 5 points.

7. The team that has the most points at the end of the game (however long the class has earned to play the Strongest Link) wins.

8. Use easy to moderate difficulty items in the beginning so that the Strongest Link will become reinforcing for many students to play, placing skilled players in each group.

FORM 2.2

List of Possible Earned Activities (Continued)

<u>Break Cards</u>

1. 3-minute break card
2. 5-minute break card
3. 7-minute break card
4. 8-minute break card
5. 10-minute break card

<u>Communication Time</u>

1. Passing a note to a friend time—5 minutes
2. Passing a note to a friend time—7 minutes
3. Passing a note to a friend time—10 minutes

<u>The Strongest Link—Academic Game</u>

1. Game—10 minutes
2. Game—20 minutes
3. Game—30 minutes

<u>TGIF</u>

1. 5 minutes toward Friday party
2. 8 minutes toward Friday party
3. 10 minutes toward Friday party

_____ **FORM 2.3** _____

Classroom Rule Violations Chart

(For Seat Work and/or Lesson Presentation)

1. Talking (or interrupting teacher) without permission
2. Being out-of-seat without permission
3. Disturbing or distracting others by noises, talk, or motor activity

---- **FORM 2.4** ----

The Good Behavior Board Game Rules

- Follow the Good Behavior Rules when doing your class work.

- The timer is set for a 10-minute interval.

- Each rule violation of any student is recorded on the Rule Violation Chart for that interval.

- When the timer goes off, the class icon moves up one spot on the board, if it has reached its goal, such as fewer than 6 rule violations for that interval.

- The timer is reset for another 10-minute interval.

- When the class reaches a treasure box on the game board, one student selects a ticket from the treasure box, the entire class gets that activity or event at a teacher-designated time that day or the next.

- Each day, the team begins again at the start of the game board.

── FORM 2.5 ──

Rule Violation Chart—Baseline

Date: _____

Instructional Period: _____

10-Minute Intervals   Tallies of Rule Violations

First

Second

Third

Fourth

Fifth

Sixth

Seventh

Eighth

Ninth

FORM 2.6

Rule Violation Chart

Good Behavior Goal: _____

Date: _____

Instructional Period: _____

10-Minute Interval	Tallies of Rule Violations	Met Goal?
First		
Second		
Third		
Fourth		
Fifth		
Sixth		
Seventh		
Eighth		
Ninth		

Number of successful intervals / Total number of intervals: _____

FORM 2.7

Weekly Summary Sheet

Week of _____

Instructional Period(s): _____

	Number of Successful Intervals	Total Number of Intervals
Monday		
Tuesday		
Wednesday		
Thursday		
Friday		

3

Behavioral Contracting

BRIEF DESCRIPTION

In some cases, the disruptive behavior of only a few students is of concern to the teacher. The teacher may feel comfortable with his general classroom management strategy for the class as a whole, but he may need specific strategies for a few individual students. Behavioral contracting is well suited for these circumstances (Homme, 1970; Kelly & Stokes, 1982; Main & Munro, 1977). A behavioral contract is a simple arrangement that links an individual child's behavior with long-term rewards or incentives (Miller & Kelley, 1994; Murphy, 1988). Behavior contracts usually cover a long period of time (e.g., 2, 3, or 4 weeks). The length of time is called the *contract period*.

The child's behavior is evaluated daily against a certain behavior standard (called a *daily behavioral standard*). The contract specifies the number of days the child must achieve the behavior standard (called the *contract terms*). If the child satisfies the contract terms, a reinforcer specified in the contract is provided. The contract also specifies when, where, and how much of the reinforcer is delivered to the child. Once a contract has been met, the teacher can write a new behavioral contract to cover another period of time. Therefore, over the course of a term or semester, several successive contracts may be written. For example, the teacher may write a behavioral contract for the first 2 weeks, another behavioral contract for the next 3 weeks, a third for the following 3 weeks, and so on. See Form 3.1 for a teacher-designated plan.

TERMS

daily behavioral standard the level of disruptive behavior that is considered acceptable for a given day.

contract period the length of time the contract is enforced.

contract terms the behavioral obligations of the child and the reinforcers that are earned if the contract terms are met. It specifies how many times (or a percentage of the total) that the child must achieve the daily behavioral standard over the contract period.

APPARATUS

A hypothetical sample behavioral contract is presented in Figure 3.1 (a blank sample is found in Form 3.2). The contract illustrates the basic components of the behavioral contracting method. Within the contract, the teacher identifies the behavior standard for each day (e.g., 2 or fewer occurrences of verbal abuse). The teacher also identifies the number of days in the contract period that the child will have to meet the behavior standard (e.g., 6 of 10 days). Finally, contingent upon the child meeting the contract terms, the reinforcers that will be delivered, as well as when and how they will be delivered, are specified (e.g., allowed to play with a Game Boy during recess). The child (if applicable) would have a copy of the contract, along with the teacher.

Behavioral Contract

Target child: R. F.

Class: Ms. Ryback's fourth grade

Target child behavior: Verbal abuse—any occurrence of yelling, screaming above a conversation tone, or profanity directed toward other students while on playground.

Daily behavioral standard: Two or fewer occurrences in a day (incorporates several playground periods).

Length of contract: 2 weeks

Contract terms: Must achieve behavior standard 6 of 10 days (not including absences) during contract period. Absences extend time period until 10 school days have been accrued.

Teacher obligations: If R. F. meets contract terms, Ms. Ryback will allow R. F. to bring his portable video game to school within 4 days of meeting contract terms to play with during a recess period that day.

Criteria for new contract:

1. Meeting current contract terms—new contract will be drawn up the following day.

2. Failing to meet contract terms—a minimum of a 4-day wait period before new contract is drawn up.

FIGURE 3.1
A Sample Behavioral Contract

BASELINE MEASUREMENT

Baseline data on the frequency of the target disruptive behavior should be collected for at least a contract term. Form 3.3 at the end of this chapter can be used for baseline and intervention phases.

PROCEDURES

1. Identify the target children.
2. Identify the target behavior, either undesirable behavior (to decrease), such as disruptive behavior, or desirable behavior (to increase), such as the number of times the hand is raised appropriately.
3. Collect baseline data on the frequency of the behavior for each target child.
4. Based on the baseline data, set the behavior standard (e.g., frequency of behavior deemed acceptable for each day) and designate how the behavior will be monitored.

5. With the child, set the contract terms of the behavioral contract, indicating how many days the behavior standard must be achieved within the contract period.

6. Designate what reinforcers the child would like to earn as a function of meeting the contract terms.

7. Implement the behavior monitoring system (see Form 3.3).

8. If the child reaches the behavior standard for the day, check it on the contract chart. If the child meets the contract terms at the end of the contract period, deliver the reinforcer at the designated time and place.

9. If the child does not meet the obligations of the contract, end the current contract and consider writing a new one after a break of one to several days (so as not to teach the child to break contracts indiscriminately).

HOW IT WORKS

The utility of the behavioral contract is in its ability to target children who are having more difficulty than the rest of the class. The behavior standard must be determined through baseline data and set so that the children will achieve success with the first several contracts. The teacher may need to be content initially with a higher behavior standard than with the ultimate target goal.

As the child achieves success and experiences the reward, she will be more motivated to behave appropriately to meet the contracts that are subsequently set up. The teacher then shapes the child's level of disruptive behavior to lower numbers of occurrences by gradually moving the behavior standard closer to the desired goal. For example, after a child meets the contract terms by staying under 3 disruptive incidents per day for 8 of 10 days, the next behavioral contract might require no more than 2 disruptive incidents per day for 6 out of the next 10 days.

ADDITIONAL CONSIDERATIONS

Inaccurate Baseline Data

Occasionally, the baseline data collected might underestimate the level of disruptive behavior. Therefore, the teacher might set a higher initial behavior standard than what the child is capable of performing. The teacher should suspect that this is the case if the child doesn't succeed in the first several behavioral contracts. If the child misses the first few contracts for whatever reason, reevaluate the behavior standard on the basis of the child's performance on the last several behavioral contracts. Then, establish a new behavior standard that is more within reach of the child.

Strengthen Reinforcers

If a child fails the first few behavioral contracts, another reason may be that the reinforcer being used is not potent enough. In most cases, when children are involved in deciding the reinforcer they are to earn, potency is usually not the issue. However, if the child either is not interested in that reinforcer or can get it elsewhere without having to meet a contract, it may not be sufficiently attractive to motivate the child. In those cases, consider finding another reinforcer to use in the contract.

Application for Aggressive Behavior

For behaviors like aggression, one may set the behavior standard at 0 occurrences for a given day or time period so that nonaggression is reinforced. However, some children may be unable to meet contract terms that require 5 days of nonaggression. In those cases, the contracts can be designed to provide an achievable standard. For example, the contract terms may require the child to achieve only a certain proportion of days or time periods with 0 occurrences to enable him to meet with success. If a child is aggressive once or twice a day, the behavior standard might be set at 0 occurrences for 2-hour blocks during the day (e.g., three 2-hour blocks during a school day). The contract terms might require the child to meet the standard at least 2 of 3 blocks per day for 4 consecutive days. This would be a more reasonable standard for this child, in contrast to requiring 5 straight days of 0 occurrences of aggression. Remember, when setting the behavior standard and the contract terms, be guided by the baseline data!

HYPOTHETICAL EXAMPLE

Dealing With Physical Aggression

Renaldo has had a history of physical aggression toward other children. The school has previously attempted out-of-school suspensions, in-school suspensions, parent conferences, and time-outs. However, none of these efforts has resulted in a change in Renaldo's aggressive behavior. Mrs. Ralph decides to implement a behavioral contract for Renaldo. She sets up a behavioral contract that gives Renaldo points during time periods in which he refrains from aggressive behavior. She defines *aggression* as hitting another child. She decides to observe Renaldo for a 1-week period to collect baseline data. He engages in aggressive behavior between 0 and 2 occurrences per day.

Renaldo also pushes and shoves other children. She collects baseline data on his rate of pushing and shoving for a week. Renaldo is pushing and shoving other children between one and four times a day.

Using this information, Mrs. Ralph sets the behavioral standard for a 1-hour block. Renaldo will earn 5 points if he does not engage in any aggressive behavior or pushing and shoving other children during that time period. Therefore, the school day is divided into 5 hour-long blocks. The first contract period is for 1 week. At the end of the week, if Renaldo has earned 15 or more points each day for all 5 days, he is allowed to have 20 more minutes of extra recess on Friday afternoon (along with his classmates).

Mrs. Ralph implements the plan after reviewing it with Renaldo. The program is a success! He earns extra recess for the first 4 behavioral contracts. Mrs. Ralph then changes the contract terms to require Renaldo

Notes

to earn 20 points a day each day of the week to earn extra Friday recess. She hopes that within 3 months Renaldo will be able to refrain from hitting, pushing, or shoving other children for several weeks at a time.

HYPOTHETICAL EXAMPLE

Increasing Appropriate Behavior

Sarah has started coming late to class after recess period. Each day there are four recess periods, and Sarah is late coming in from recess after at least two of the four periods. On some days she is late all four times. Mrs. Wildman has attempted to intervene by discussing this with Sarah and her parents, as well as constantly reminding Sarah to come back to class on time. None of these efforts has worked.

Mrs. Wildman decides to set up a behavioral contract with Sarah. With the baseline data indicating between 2 and 4 tardies, Mrs. Wildman sets the daily behavioral standard of coming in from recess on time 2 or more times. Each time Sarah is on time, she will receive a check, with a maximum of 4 earned checks per day. Sarah must achieve the daily behavioral standard on 11 out of 15 days to meet the contract terms. Absences are not included in this contract. *Being tardy* is defined as failing to be in the classroom after the class door is closed (signifying the end of recess). Mrs. Wildman will blow the whistle twice, signaling the time for all children to line up in front of the door to the classroom. A minute later, the students in line come inside the classroom.

Mrs. Wildman goes over the behavioral contract with Sarah, and Sarah agrees to the terms. If Sarah meets the contract terms, she will be given a 1-hour music and dance party with all her classmates on the next Friday in which the contract is met. If she does not meet the contract, 5 days must elapse before a new contract is written up. Additionally, if Sarah does not come in on time for a given recess period, Mrs. Wildman will simply go out and get Sarah and bring her into class. She will not get a check for that period.

Sarah meets the first set of contract terms, earning a dance party that Friday. Mrs. Wildman continues the use of behavioral contracts to facilitate Sarah's coming in from recess on time. After 4 additional behavioral contracts, with 3 of them successful, Mrs. Wildman sets the behavior standard at 4 out of 4 recesses being on time for 10 out of 15 days. The goal of being on time every day is now a possibility.

WHAT IF?

- How did behavioral contracting work for Sarah's tardy behavior? Do you think selecting a dance party is a good idea for getting Sarah's peers behind her efforts to come in from recess?

- How valuable is it for Mrs. Ralph to precisely specify the target behavior on the behavioral contract? What might happen if a behavioral contract is written for a target behavior problem as vague as "good behavior"?

- How can behavioral contracting be used to develop a consistent approach between home and school with a child? What might be the role of the parents?

FORMS

3.1 Behavioral Contract: Teacher-Designated Plan—Teacher uses this form for written plan.

3.2 Sample Blank Behavioral Contract Form—For an individual student. Posted and available to student. Teacher can fill in blanks when writing a contract for student.

3.3 Daily Frequency of Behavior Chart—Teacher can use this data sheet for two target behaviors, if needed, just circling next highest number with each occurrence.

Notes

FORM 3.1

Behavioral Contract: Teacher-Designated Plan

Target child: _____

Target behavior(s)—(define each behavior): _____

_____

Contract period: _____

Baseline data across 8 days (designate either *frequency* or *proportion*):

(1) _____   (6) _____

(2) _____   (7) _____

(3) _____   (8) _____

(4) _____   Mean frequency: _____

(5) _____   Range: _____

Target behavioral goal: _____

Daily behavioral standard: _____

Contract terms: _____

Criteria for altering contract terms: _____

Reinforcer for meeting contract terms: _____

Who will implement plan: _____

Parental consent (if needed): _____

Administrator signature: _____

FORM 3.2

Sample Behavioral Contract

Target child: _____

Class: _____

Target child behavior: _____

Daily behavioral standard: _____

Length of contract: _____

Contract terms: _____

Teacher obligations: _____

Criteria for new contract: _____

FORM 3.3

Daily Frequency of Behavior Chart

Child's name: _____

Contract period: _____

Contract terms: _____

Target behavior 1: _____

    1   2   3   4   5   6   7   8   9   10   11   12

Target behavior 2: _____

    1   2   3   4   5   6   7   8   9   10   11   12

4

Individual Disruptive Incident Barometer

BRIEF DESCRIPTION

The individual disruptive incident barometer program enables the teacher to monitor the occurrence of a child's target disruptive behaviors by plotting each occurrence on the individual child's disruptive incident barometer. Loss of points from an initial stipend, as a contingency, has been found effective (DuPaul, Guevremont, & Barkley, 1992; Kaufman & O'Leary, 1972; McLaughlin & Malaby, 1972; Truhlicka, McLaughlin, & Swain, 1998). Each time the child engages in a target disruptive behavior, the barometer is moved down one level (see Form 4.1). A behavior standard is identified through baseline data to determine the acceptable level of a disruptive behavior. The behavior standard is depicted as a solid line drawn between two levels on the individual disruptive incident barometer. If the child stays at or below this target level, reinforcement occurs at the end of the period (or day, depending on the length of time it is used).

The disruptive incident barometer is a visually pleasing display that monitors the rate of disruptive behaviors of given children. The visual display (on a bulletin board or poster, or on the child's desk in an erasable medium) presents a barometer with numbered levels (for younger children, you can use letters or different colors). Each level corresponds to an act of disruptive behavior. As a child engages in a disruptive behavior, the teacher circles or marks the next level, moving the child closer to the behavior standard or to the point at which the child loses the reinforcer. A solid line drawn between two levels indicates the behavior standard.

TERMS

> **behavior standard** the level of disruptive behavior that is considered acceptable. The standard identifies the target level for the barometer and the rate at or above which the child earns the reinforcer.

APPARATUS

The barometer featured in Column A in Figure 4.1 illustrates a plan that provides for 10 levels (i.e., 10 occurrences of disruptive behavior for a given period). The behavior standard is at or above Level 7 (the child must not engage in disruptive behavior more than 4 times). The barometer featured in Column B illustrates a system with 20 levels, with the standard for reinforcement at or above Level 13. Obviously, the longer the period of time the individual disruptive incident barometer program is in effect (e.g., half an hour versus 3 hours), the more levels are needed for the barometer.

The disruptive incident barometer itself can be illustrated in several ways:

- Paper chart on the child's desk
- Individual laminated chart on each child's desk
- Individual laminated chart on teacher's desk

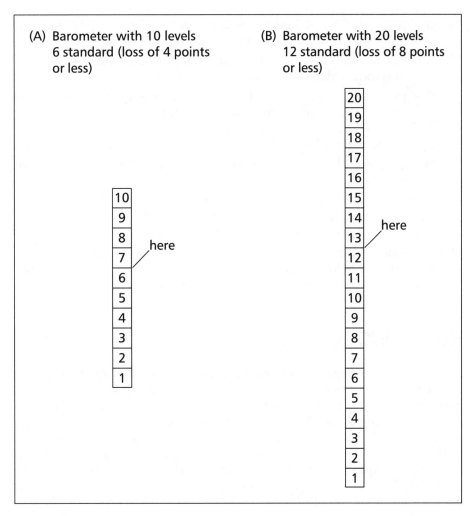

(A) Barometer with 10 levels
    6 standard (loss of 4 points
    or less)

(B) Barometer with 20 levels
    12 standard (loss of 8 points
    or less)

FIGURE 4.1
Disruptive Incident Barometer

BASELINE MEASUREMENT

Use the barometer apparatus for 5 to 8 days in the target time period to collect data on the rate of disruptive behavior for each child who will be in the
program. On the basis of these data, the behavior standard can be determined. Form 4.2 at the end of this chapter can be used for this purpose.

PROCEDURES

1. Identify the target children.
2. Identify the target disruptive behaviors, that is, the disruptive behavior
   that will result in the loss of a level.
3. Collect baseline data on the rate of disruptive behaviors of the target
   children or entire class for 4 to 7 days (if representative of other days in
   terms of levels of occurrence).

4. Designate the time periods you will implement the disruptive incident barometer program (or across the entire day).

5. Identify the initial behavior standard and what reinforcer will be earned if the child meets the behavior standard.

6. Design the disruptive incident barometer with the appropriate number of levels and draw a line below the behavior standard level (e.g., a solid dark line between 4 and 5 on a chart with 10 points indicates that the child earns the reinforcer if he or she doesn't lose more than 6 points).

7. When a target disruptive behavior occurs, move the barometer down one by coloring or circling the next highest level.

8. At end of a designated period (e.g., at end of 1 hour, 2 hours, before noon, or the entire day), determine whether the child achieved the standard and deliver the reinforcer if appropriate.

9. Continue to implement the individual disruptive incident barometer, adjusting the behavior standard to require a lower frequency of disruptive behavior to achieve the desired behavior standard.

HOW IT WORKS

The individual disruptive incident barometer sets a behavior standard for an acceptable level of disruptive behavior, and, when achieved, results in a powerful reinforcer being delivered. It enables the teacher to set an initial standard for an individual child that is achievable (given that baseline data were used to determine the initial standard). Once the child achieves the initial standard, the standard can become progressively more stringent, reducing disruptive behavior to desirable levels gradually but systematically. The barometer's use in research studies, as a technique termed *differential reinforcement of low rates of behavior*, has been extremely successful (Dietz & Repp, 1973; Zwald & Gresham, 1982).

ADDITIONAL CONSIDERATIONS

When a Child Falls Below the Barometer Line

In some cases, when a child falls below the barometer line, indicating her loss of the reinforcer for that time period, he or she may become more difficult until the next barometer is put into place (e.g., the child loses the chance to earn the reinforcer at 2:30 P.M. because he or she went past the barometer line at 11:45 A.M.). This can be handled in any of several effective and acceptable ways. However, a way that is unacceptable is to change the behavior standard, or the previous recording of disruptive behavior, as a function of the child's lack of success in achieving a behavior standard on a given day. The changing of the behavior standard must be made before the beginning of the barometer program for that day or period. Don't change the recording simply because the child failed; that sends the message that when the child fails to generate enough self-control on a given day, we will alter the standard. If this is done often, the child's behavior will be less likely to change systematically; rather, it will appear that the teacher's behavior changes to accommodate whatever the student does.

One requirement for handling a failure to achieve the behavior standard is the continuance of the program, with the teacher riding out the temporary increase in disruptive behavior. The teacher may have a tough time that day, but with a new barometer program the next day or period the child has a whole new chance to reach the standard and will certainly remember what happened the previous day after she failed to regulate her behavior (i.e., the child will learn that there is a consequence for not demonstrating the appropriate behavior).

This temporary "storm" can be lessened by designing shorter time periods for the barometer program. For example, if the period for the barometer program was initially set at the whole day, the teacher might consider having 2 barometer programs, one in the morning and a new program in the afternoon. Then, the child could start fresh each half-day. Or, a new barometer program could begin every 2 hours. The designation of the length of time for the barometer program is best done by consulting the data and the child's behavior.

Another method for lessening the effect of the child's disruptive behavior is to use a graded system. For example, on a 20-level barometer system, the child earns 5 extra minutes of recess time if he or she stays above Level 14, 3 extra minutes if he or she stays above Level 11, and 1 extra minute if he or she stays above Level 8. This provides an incentive on any given day to keep trying.

Inaccurate Baseline Data

Occasionally, the baseline data might underestimate the level of disruptive behavior. Therefore, the teacher might set a lower initial behavior standard for the disruptive behavior barometer than the child is capable of achieving. For example, a behavior standard set at 4 might be unreasonable if the baseline data should have revealed more than 8 occurrences per day. Suspect that this is the case if the child doesn't succeed with the first several barometers. Reevaluate the behavior standard on the basis of the child's performance on the last several barometers (e.g., the child stayed below 8 incidents in the last 3 barometers). Then, establish a new behavior standard to be more within reach of the child.

Strengthen Reinforcers

If a child fails to access the reinforcer in the first few barometers, another reason may be that the reinforcer being used is not potent enough. In most cases, when children are involved in deciding the reinforcer they are to earn, potency is usually not the issue. However, if the child either is not interested in that reinforcer or can get it elsewhere without having to meet the barometer standard, it may not be sufficiently attractive to motivate the child. In those cases, consider finding another reinforcer to use with the barometer program.

HYPOTHETICAL EXAMPLE

Reducing Teasing

R. K. teases several other students in the class. It is obviously annoying to the children being teased, as well as to other children in the vicinity. Mr. Baros is concerned about this behavior, both for its effect on the other children as well as on R. K. He has talked to R. K. multiple times about how his teasing hurts the other children, but this does not deter him from teasing children the next day. Mr. Baros has also used time-outs, but without success. He notes that R. K. likes physical education class and enjoys helping the instructor. After talking with the instructor, Mr. Baros obtains his consent to use a special reinforcer for R. K. if he meets a behavioral goal.

Mr. Baros sets up a disruptive incident barometer after obtaining the following baseline frequency of R. K.'s teasing across 5 days: 9, 12, 15, 6, and 10. He designs a disruptive incident barometer that goes up to 20 and sets the behavior standard between 10 and 11. Each time R. K. teases someone, he will lose a point, starting from 1 point. R. K. can lose up to 10 points and still achieve the standard for that day. However, if R. K. teases 11 or more times that day, he does not earn the reinforcer. Mr. Baros explains to R. K. that he will remove a point each time that R. K. engages in teasing behavior. Mr. Baros is careful to point out what constitutes teasing behavior and suggests alternative things he might say (e.g., compliments or questions). If R. K. meets the behavior standard for all the days before the next physical education period, he will be allowed to help the instructor for 10 minutes during the next class. (Physical education class meets twice a week, Wednesday and Friday.)

WHAT IF?

- What might happen if R. K.'s teasing of other children is socially reinforced by a select group of peers? Would an individual disruptive incident barometer work to decrease his teasing behavior? Why or why not?

- What might Mr. Baros have done to directly increase the use of compliments or questions on the part of R. K.?

- What are the differences in the types of disruptive classroom behavior with elementary school students versus junior and senior high students?

FORMS

4.1 Individual Disruptive Incident Barometer Agreement—Can be posted for child's view.

4.2 Individual Disruptive Incident Barometer Program: Teacher-Designated Plan—Teacher uses this form for written plan.

— FORM 4.1 —

Individual Disruptive Incident Barometer Agreement

Rule: Whenever you, _____ [child's name] engage in the following

disruptive behavior(s): _____, you move one level down on the

disruptive incident barometer. You lose a level each time you engage in _____

_____. If the barometer stays above the solid line, drawn between

_____ and _____, you earn _____.

Disruptive Behaviors

1.

2.

3.

4.

Remember, being considerate of the teacher and your classmates and following class rules pays off!

—— **FORM 4.2** ——

Individual Disruptive Incident Barometer Program: Teacher-Designated Plan

Target child: _____

Target disruptive behavior(s): _____

_____

Designated time period(s): _____

Number of levels of incident barometer: _____

Present baseline data across 5 days/sessions:

1. _____

2. _____

3. _____

4. _____

5. _____

Target behavioral standard: _____

Initial behavioral standard (number of levels that can be lost before losing

reinforcement): _____

Line drawn between which two numbers: _____

Criteria for adjusting standard up: _____

Criteria for adjusting standard down: _____

Reinforcer earned for achieving behavioral standard: _____

Who will implement plan? _____

Parental consent (if needed): _____

Administrator's signature: _____

5

Signal Time-Out for Minor Disruptive Behavior

BRIEF DESCRIPTION

To address minor disruptive behaviors, this program combines a signal time-out with a reinforcement plan for on-task behaviors (e.g., the beeper system discussed in chapter 8). Unlike the removal time-out described in chapter 6, the signal time-out procedure does not entail removing the children from the area or classroom (Foxx & Shapiro, 1978; Salend & Gordon, 1987; Yeager & McLaughlin, 1995). Rather, the children remain in their seats. However, they cannot earn any points during the signal time-out period.

The signal time-out period is specified by the placement of a badge, sticker, or card on the student's desk or tag board for a designated minimum time period. In the initial empirical study, a badge was used (Foxx & Shapiro, 1978). However, if the child continues the disruptive behavior during the time-out, the time period can be extended until the child quiets down. If more severe disruptive behavior occurs during the signal time-out period, the teacher may use the removal time-out procedure to avoid jeopardizing the safety of other students or their learning experience.

TERMS

minor disruptive behaviors behaviors that do not cause a major disruption to the learning environment or do not present a dangerous condition to the child or others.

APPARATUS

The specific form of the signal time-out needs to be designated. In some cases, it can be a card placed on the student's desk or a tag board with a list of students on signal time-out at any given time. With young children, a sticker or badge can be used. In addition, an oven timer should be used to keep track of the length of time the child remains in the signal time-out. Use Form 5.1 at the end of this chapter to delineate the signal time-out program for report purposes.

BASELINE MEASUREMENT

The disruptive behaviors that produce a signal time-out need to be delineated (see Form 5.2). Each behavior could be coded and scored as to its frequency of occurrence. An illustration of a data collection sheet with hypothetical baseline data is shown in Figure 5.1.

PROCEDURES

1. Define the target disruptive behaviors that constitute minor disruptive behavior (e.g., getting out of seat, talking out, talking to peers, or making unnecessary noise).

Frequency of Disruptive Behavior Data Sheet

Child's name (or entire class): Entire fourth-grade class
Period: Reading/Language Arts 10–11 A.M.

Behavior/Date	6–7	6–8	6–9	6–10	6–11	Total/Week
(1) Unauthorized talking	~~JHT~~ ll	lll	~~JHT~~ l	~~JHT~~	~~JHT~~	26
(2) Out-of-seat occurrences	lll	~~JHT~~ ll	lll	~~JHT~~	~~JHT~~ l	24

FIGURE 5.1
A Sample Data Sheet for the Frequency of Disruptive Behavior

2. Implement the beeper system to reward on-task behavior and collect baseline data on the rate of minor disruptive behaviors.

3. Specify the minimum signal time-out period.

4. When a minor disruptive behavior occurs, the signal (e.g., a badge, sticker, or ribbon) is placed at the child's desk or on the tag board or, in the case of younger children, on their person.

5. Set the timer for the minimum signal time-out length.

6. The child does not receive points for being on task during the signal time-out period.

7. If minor disruptive behaviors continue during the signal time-out period, do not remove the signal until the child is quiet.

8. If more severe disruptive behavior occurs during the time-out period, use the removal time-out program (discussed in chapter 6) for severe disruptive behavior.

9. When the signal time-out period is over, remove the signal time-out. The child can then begin earning points for being on task.

HOW IT WORKS

Signal time-outs can be effective by removing the opportunity to earn points for the appropriate classroom behavior (i.e., being on task). If the points can be traded in for powerful incentives, the child will be motivated to stay on task and do his or her work. By reinforcing on-task behavior as part of the overall plan, the use of the signal time-out for disruptive behavior increases the students' motivation to engage in the appropriate on-task behavior and avoid getting a signal time-out.

ADDITIONAL CONSIDERATIONS

Setting a Minimum Signal Time-Out Length

The minimum length of the signal time-out should be a period of time that would include the student losing at least 1 opportunity to earn points (i.e., at least 1 beep). Therefore, if the beeps average once every 3 minutes, the minimum length should be set for at least 3 minutes. While that doesn't ensure that at least 1 beep will occur in the signal time-out (because some intervals between beeps may be longer than 3 minutes), it does provide a good basis for the minimum time-out period.

Altering the Density of Beeps on the Beeper System

In using the signal time-out procedure, if the rate of disruptive behavior does not decrease, consider increasing the number of beeps that occur during the period(s). This would make points more frequently available and provide a greater opportunity to catch the children being on task and not engaging in disruptive behavior. Also, examine the reinforcers that back up the points to determine whether these might be changed or enhanced to act as more powerful incentives for on-task behavior.

HYPOTHETICAL EXAMPLE

Group Application for "Chatter"

A third-grade teacher wants to decrease the frequency of chatter among students during the reading period. Part of her problem is her inability to detect all who are talking. She decides to implement a group plan for a 3-minute signal time-out along with the beeper system. These 3 minutes would ensure that at least 1 and possibly 2 to 3 beeps would occur during the signal time-out period. Contingent upon class chatter reaching a detectable level, a yellow card will be placed on the teacher's desk for everyone to see. The oven timer will be set for 3 minutes. During this time, no student will receive points when the beeps occur. If the class is quiet for the 3 minutes, the yellow card is removed and all the students can begin earning points for being on task when the beep sounds.

WHAT IF?

- Would the signal time-out program be better suited for younger or older students? Why?
- What would happen if the time-out program were used without the beeper system? What would be the effect on disruptive behavior—would it decrease? Why or why not?

FORMS

5.1 Signal Time-Out Program: Teacher-Designated Plan—Teacher uses this form for written plan.

5.2 Signal Time-Out Policy—Can be posted.

FORM 5.1

Signal Time-Out Program:
Teacher-Designated Plan

Target child: _____

Target disruptive behavior(s): _____

_____

Designated time period(s): _____

Baseline data across 5 days/sessions (designate the frequency of disruptive behavior):

1. _____

2. _____

3. _____

4. _____

5. _____

Target goal (average frequency of disruptive behavior across five sessions): _____

Signal time-out mechanism (e.g., card, badge, sticker): _____

Signal time-out period: _____

Who will implement plan? _____

Parental consent (if needed): _____

Administrator's signature: _____

FORM 5.2

Signal Time-Out Policy

You can earn points for being on task, doing your work, or attending to me while I am teaching. However, if you engage in the following disruptive behaviors:

1. _____

2. _____

3. _____

4. _____

you will lose the opportunity to earn points for at least a _____-minute period. I will signal this by _____. If you are quiet during this period, the _____ will be removed at the end, and you can begin earning points again for being on task. If you do not follow the rules for time-out, your time will be extended until you follow the rules. *Remember: Do your work—it pays off!*

6

Removal Time-Out for Severe Disruptive and Aggressive Behavior

BRIEF DESCRIPTION

A traditional time-out (i.e., removal from an area or class) is often used in an attempt to decrease disruptive and aggressive behavior. However, in many classrooms, time-outs may not be effective, particularly if the child sees them as a way to get out of doing classwork. In spite of this possibility, when disruptive behaviors are of such a nature that the safety of the child or other children is of concern or the learning environment is disrupted to a substantial degree, the child's removal from the area may be a high priority. The removal time-out program combines the time-out with an existing plan for rewarding appropriate behaviors in situations in which the child needs to be removed.

Children receive points for being on task during classroom instruction via the beeper system or the task engagement program (see part 3 for both plans). If severe disruptive or aggressive behavior is exhibited, the child is removed from the area or class (see Form 6.1). During this removal time-out period, the child does not receive points for being on task as the beeps occur. The time-out period is specified in terms of a minimal amount of time the child is removed (e.g., 2 minutes). If the child continues being disruptive in the time-out area, the time-out is extended until the child demonstrates that he or she is ready to rejoin the class activity in an appropriate manner.

TERMS

severe disruptive behavior behavior that creates a dangerous classroom situation or halts instruction to the class, in the judgment of the teacher.

APPARATUS

A time-out area needs to be designated. This area should be void of materials or objects the child could use to entertain himself or herself. In addition, the Removal Time-Out Tracking Sheet (see Form 6.2) should be posted near the time-out area to keep track of each removal time-out as well as the length of time the child remains in time-out. In some cases, when dealing with extremely disruptive or aggressive behavior, a place that can be supervised by school personnel outside the classroom may have to be used. Site administrators should be brought into the design of this strategy.

BASELINE MEASUREMENT

A simple frequency count of severe disruptive behaviors needs to be taken for a 5- to 8-day period (see Form 6.3, the Frequency Chart). The teacher wants to distinguish between severe disruptive behavior (which results in the child's removal from the area or classroom) and less severe disruptive behaviors, which can be handled with techniques not requiring removal (see the signal time-out program in chapter 5). More severe disruptive behaviors that could (or should) result in the removal of the child are (a) attempted or actual physically aggressive behavior; (b) loud, verbally abusive behavior toward a teacher or peers in the classroom; (c) property destruction; and (d) any other behaviors that create a dangerous situation or significantly halt instruction to the class (should be determined a priori).

PROCEDURES

1. Define the disruptive behaviors that constitute severely disruptive or aggressive behaviors (e.g., verbally abusive statements, profanity, aggression, tantrums, and refusal to return to seat).
2. Implement the beeper system for on-task behavior and collect baseline data on the rates of severe disruptive behaviors for the students being studied.
3. Specify the minimum time-out period.
4. When a severe disruptive behavior occurs, guide the child to the time-out area with no work.
5. Set the timer for the minimum period of time.
6. If the child continues to be disruptive in time-out, do not release him or her when timer goes off.
7. Once the child calms down in the time-out area, set the timer for a short time (e.g., 30 seconds).
8. If the child is quiet for that short time, release him or her back to class to begin work.
9. The child does not receive any points while in the removal time-out.
10. The child can begin earning points once he or she returns and begins work.
11. Another occurrence of severe disruptive behavior, no matter how soon after reentry to class, results in the repetition of the previous process.

HOW IT WORKS

Removal time-out is used for extreme disruptive behavior in the classroom, where its continuance either significantly hinders the learning environment or jeopardizes the physical safety of the target child or other children in the class. The removal from class preserves the safety of and the learning environment for the rest of the class. By combining the removal time-out procedure with a reinforcement plan (e.g., the beeper system), this program increases the motivation of the child to want to stay in the activity. Otherwise, the child may not mind being removed from the activity or classroom. It is therefore *imperative* that a plan from part 3 be used in conjunction with the removal time-out program to minimize the attractiveness of being removed from class activities.

ADDITIONAL CONSIDERATION

If the child demonstrates extreme dangerous behaviors (e.g., assaultive behaviors toward other students or the teacher), additional precautions may need to be taken to implement this time-out. Crisis management techniques may need to be invoked if the child's behavior reaches a level at which the safety of the teacher or other students is a primary concern. If the child becomes assaultive during an escort to time-out, this plan should be reevaluated by persons who are trained in applied behavior analysis.

HYPOTHETICAL EXAMPLE

Removal Time-Out for Verbal Abuse

Ms. Jones is concerned about her student Raul, who becomes extremely verbally abusive to other students and the teacher between 0 and 1 time per day. During these episodes, he may not be able to settle down for some time and the classroom environment is disrupted. Ms. Jones decides to implement a 5-minute removal time-out in conjunction with the beeper system for reinforcing on-task behavior. During this 5-minute period, Raul will miss at least 1 and possibly 2 to 3 beeps. When Raul becomes verbally abusive, Ms. Jones will take Raul to the time-out area. Her aide will remain with him until he stays at least 5 minutes in the time-out area and is quiet and calm for the last 2 minutes. The aide sets the timer when he is escorted to the time-out area. When the time-out period is over, he is brought back to the class to begin working on previously assigned work and then can receive points for being on task when the beep sounds.

If Raul does not go to time-out willingly, he does not earn points during the time he should have been placed in time-out. Ms. Jones has been trained in crisis management techniques and knows what to do should Raul become assaultive. Additionally, a behavior analyst will be consulted at that point for possible changes in the plan.

WHAT IF?

- Do you think teachers should be trained in crisis management techniques? Why or why not? Is it more important for teachers of older students to have this training?

- What criteria would you need for a removal time-out? Would you consider such a policy at all, in conjunction with a behavioral plan that rewards the appropriate behavior?

FORMS

6.1 Removal Time-Out Policy—Can be posted.

6.2 Removal Time-Out Tracking Sheet—To be filled out each time a student is removed to the time-out area; to be used as documentation for its use.

6.3 Frequency Chart—Teacher enters date for each row and then circles a number each time a severe disruptive behavior occurs.

6.4 Removal Time-Out Program: Teacher-Designated Plan—Teacher uses this form for written plan.

─── **FORM 6.1** ───

Removal Time-Out Policy

    If a student's behavior is serious enough to cause me to stop instruction, she or he will be removed to the time-out area (or removed from the classroom) to preserve the learning experience of others in the classroom. When the student demonstrates that she or he is ready to return to the learning experience with the rest of the class by serving _____ minutes in time-out and following the rules for time-out (1) _____ (2) _____ (3) _____, she or he will be returned and can begin earning points.

    Try to control your behavior by refraining from the following behaviors _____ _____ so I don't have to step in. Everyone can learn self-control. Practice it each day.

FORM 6.2

Removal Time-Out Tracking Sheet

Week of _____

	Date	Student	Time entered	Time released	Comments
1.	_____	_____	_____	_____	_____
2.	_____	_____	_____	_____	_____
3.	_____	_____	_____	_____	_____
4.	_____	_____	_____	_____	_____
5.	_____	_____	_____	_____	_____
6.	_____	_____	_____	_____	_____
7.	_____	_____	_____	_____	_____
8.	_____	_____	_____	_____	_____
9.	_____	_____	_____	_____	_____
10.	_____	_____	_____	_____	_____

FORM 6.3

Frequency Chart

Child: _____

Severe disruptive behaviors (list): _____

Date	1	2	3	4	5	6	7	8	9	10
_____										

Date	1	2	3	4	5	6	7	8	9	10
_____										

Date	1	2	3	4	5	6	7	8	9	10
_____										

Date	1	2	3	4	5	6	7	8	9	10
_____										

Date	1	2	3	4	5	6	7	8	9	10
_____										

Date	1	2	3	4	5	6	7	8	9	10
_____										

Date	1	2	3	4	5	6	7	8	9	10
_____										

Date	1	2	3	4	5	6	7	8	9	10
_____										

FORM 6.4

Removal Time-Out Program: Teacher-Designated Plan

Target child: _____

Reinforcement plan: Beeper system (see chapter 8 for details): _____

Severe disruptive behaviors that result in a removal time-out: _____

_____

Baseline data (sessions or days):

     1. _____

     2. _____

     3. _____

     4. _____

     5. _____

     Mean frequency

     _____

Target goal: _____

_____

Use of beeper system: _____

_____

Removal time-out plan: _____

_____

Time-out area (in class): _____

_____

Time-out area (out of class): _____

_____

Time-out period (minimum): _____

_____

Rules for time-out: _____

_____

Quiet period required: Yes   No   How long: _____

Who will implement plan? _____

_____

Parental consent (if needed): _____

_____

Administrator signature: _____

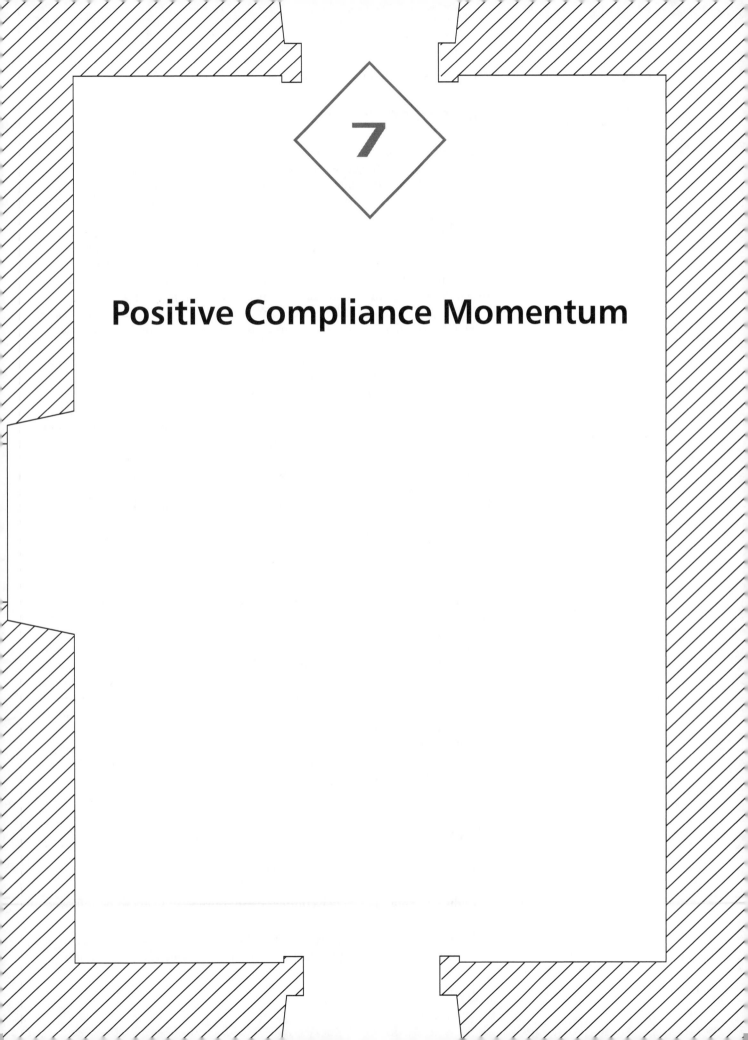

7

Positive Compliance Momentum

BRIEF DESCRIPTION

The transition to inside or outside activities can often be a difficult time for the teacher to manage the class. When some children do not comply with teacher requests to initiate the succeeding activity, transitions can interrupt the flow of instructional activities. The longer some students take to transition, the longer it takes the teacher to get the entire class involved in the next activity.

An intervention designed by researchers at Syracuse University increased several second-grade students' compliance with activity transition requests within 20 seconds of their issuance (Ardoin, Martens, & Wolfe, 1999). They termed the technique *high probability (high-p) request sequences*. In previous research, a comparable procedure termed *behavioral momentum* (Ducharme & Worling, 1996; Kennedy, Itkonen, & Lindquist, 1995; Mace et al., 1988; Singer, Singer, & Horner, 1987) proved efficacious with compliance problems in persons with developmental disabilities and young children.

In the Ardoin et al. (1999) study, children's compliance with five target requests for the morning calendar transition activity (called *target transition requests*) were measured prior to the intervention. These requests, designated as low probability (low-p) requests, were the following: (a) get in quiet position, (b) clear desk, (c) take out pencil, (d) take out calendar, and (e) return to quiet position. Such requests were very unlikely to be carried out by three of the children in this second-grade class in an acceptable time frame. The intervention consisted of interspersing several requests that are more readily followed by young children (called *high-p requests*) prior to the issuance of the low-p request sequence. The use of three high-p requests prior to the transition requests for the morning calendar activity resulted in two of the three students markedly improving their initial compliance and latency to respond.

To use this procedure during transitions, the teacher identifies a sequence of high-p requests or commands and presents these prior to the target activity transition requests. A list of potential high-p commands should be created and then tested before using them in the high-p request sequence. Commands that do not involve transition activities, such as "Everyone, touch your left elbow, touch your right ear" should be considered and tested. The commands should be of a nature that allows compliance in a short time. The high-p request sequence is presented in rapid fashion, similar to the manner requests are made in playing the children's game Simon Says. If the students in the class respond to these commands quickly and correctly, they are placed in the high-p request sequence. The use of the high-p commands in the request sequences are then gradually removed, one by one. This procedure seems particularly suited for young children at the early or middle elementary grade levels.

TERMS

low-p commands teacher commands during activity transitions that are unlikely to be followed by the student(s).

high-p commands teacher commands that are very likely to be followed by the student(s).

high-p request sequence series of high-p commands that are presented prior to the issuance of the target low-p activity transitions commands.

APPARATUS

The Transition Activity Charting form (see Form 7.1) is used to collect the data.

BASELINE MEASUREMENT

The purpose of the baseline measurement is to enable the teacher to determine whether the procedure is effective with the target student(s). Baseline data allow for a before-and-after comparison of the child(ren)'s compliance with the target activity transition requests. Although the high-p request sequence is a group strategy, only those students who demonstrate a low rate of compliance to transition requests are used in collecting baseline data. For the students initially identified by the teacher, baseline data are collected by determining the number of requests followed for the target student(s).

For purposes of data collection, the teacher will record on Form 7.1 whether the student(s) complied with all requests in the transition activity (in yes/no format). To determine whether compliance has occurred, a reasonable time interval for the student(s) to comply with each command must be identified (e.g., 20 seconds following command). The teacher's use of a verbal count is sufficient (i.e., 1, 2, 3) instead of a timing mechanism. If compliance occurs within the designated interval, the student complied with that command. If compliance does not occur within the designated interval, the student failed to comply with that command. During baseline measurements the teacher merely uses the count procedure and records the data on the form.

PROCEDURES

1. Identify time periods involving an activity transition (try not to select more than a few transitions to begin with; others can be added later).

2. Identify target low-p activity transition commands presented during these times.

3. Create a list of potential high-p commands and test them to determine whether they are more likely to be followed by the class and target students.

4. Collect baseline data on target student(s) only.

5. Designate the high-p request sequence for each target low-p command.

6. During activity transition, prior to presenting target low-p activity transition command(s), present the high-p request sequence in rapid succession.

7. Immediately present the activity transition request commands following the high-p request sequence (no time lapse between high-p sequence and first target activity transition command).

8. Continue collecting data on target low-p commands to determine whether intervention is effective.

9. Once child complies with this transition routine, begin fading the number of commands in the high probability request sequence until you can present just the target command(s).

10. If adequate results are not obtained with this procedure alone or if many students have difficulty transitioning in a reasonable time frame, consider adding the Good Behavior Board Game to this activity as an additional incentive (see Additional Considerations).

HOW IT WORKS

If you have ever played Simon Says, you may have a good feel for how this works. When playing Simon Says, it is easy to get caught up in complying with a series of quick commands. At some point, the leader of the game, "Simon," capitalizes on this momentum by getting you to comply with a command when you should not (and then summarily tosses you out of the game). The teacher builds a momentum of compliance by starting all commands with "Simon says." As the children are "trapped" in the momentum of compliance to these requests, the leader springs the unacceptable command (by not saying "Simon says") and catches a number of children off-guard. The same principle of positive compliance momentum is used in this technique.

It is important to get compliance to the high-p commands, as this momentum needs to be built prior to delivering the low-p command. This procedure involves altering the antecedent context during transition times. It can be akin to "priming the pump" on a water pump. The function of priming is to get water to flow into the pump. This technique gets the students warmed up so that they are ready to address commands that involve activity transition.

ADDITIONAL CONSIDERATIONS

Use the Good Behavior Board Game as an Additional Component

In the Ardoins et al. (1999) study, one of the three target students did not show gains in compliance to the low-p commands, despite the use of this intervention. The sole use of positive compliance momentum may not be effective in all cases, particularly if compliance is not obtained during the high-p request sequence. In those cases it may be necessary to provide a reinforcer for compliance to activity transition commands. The Good Behavior Board Game (see chapter 2) would be well suited for such as a classwide strategy.

The Good Behavior Board Game can be easily adapted for use during transition activities (in addition to its use during instructional times). The teacher should collect data on how many students comply within the time frame during the transition activity. The teacher then sets the behavior goal for moving one space on the board by delineating the number of students who need to comply during that transition. If the class meets the behavior goal for that transition, they move one space. As in the Good Behavior Board Game, the number required to comply can then be increased as a function of class performance. This "shaping process" achieves greater levels of compliance across the entire class over time. Of course, if this does not alter any one student's behavior, perhaps an individual behavioral contract is needed.

Standardize the Transition Routine

In some cases, the teacher may need to standardize transition periods into some routine in the initial phase. If the number of transition requests varies greatly from day to day for the same activity transition, the teacher might consider developing a script for such transitions. In particular, young children may need some level of routine before developing the capacity to comply with lengthy transition requests.

In some cases, transition time may be hindered by certain practices. Transition times may not be the best place to present a lecture on playground behavior. It may be best to get the transition occurring before "discussing" behavioral issues. Perhaps waiting for the scheduled recess or free time to present such a discussion may have more of an impact on their attention and subsequent change in behavior on the playground.

HYPOTHETICAL EXAMPLE

"Simon Says"

Mr. Singh is a second-grade teacher who is using the Good Behavior Board Game for several of his instructional periods. He is quite happy with the results. The only area that needs improvement is the transition back to class work from the lunch recess. Some of the students take too long getting their materials out to begin the instructional period involving language arts. He wants to use the positive compliance momentum strategy along with the Good Behavior Board Game to reduce the length of time it takes the class to get ready for his lesson.

He creates a list of possible high-p commands and tests them prior to a morning transition activity. He calls this activity "Simon Says." To make it a game, he divides the class into two groups. Through this test, he identifies high-p commands that involve simple actions. He also notes the student reaction to the Simon Says game. Compliance was excellent, even from students whose attention spans during his lectures are often lacking. This technique can certainly be used to shape up the troublesome transition time back to class work from lunch recess.

Mr. Singh begins constructing high-p request sequences such as: (a) "Everyone, raise your right hand, (b) touch your nose, and (c) raise both hands." Such a high-p request sequence will be delivered to the entire class prior to the presentation of the target transition request "get in quiet position." Praise will also be delivered intermittently for children's compliance to high- and low-p requests. Subsequent low-p requests such as "Take out your notebook and a pencil" will proceed from the momentum of compliance achieved. Additionally, Mr. Singh figures that he can use the Simon Says game to facilitate compliance to these commands because it worked so well in the previous test.

To ensure sufficient student motivation, Mr. Singh uses the Good Behavior Board Game as an additional component of his intervention.

There are four or sometimes five commands during this transition period. If the class is ready to begin the assignment by the end of the last transition request, the icon on the board will move up one space.

With the implementation of this intervention, compliance during this transition activity became drastically better. With the technique working so well, Mr. Singh began to remove the 3 preceding high-p requests individually. Over the course of 3 weeks, Mr. Singh was presenting just the transition requests during this activity, with the class readily responding.

This intervention was very effective. Days when the transition is a little slow are few and far between. Mr. Singh notes that when the class does not reach the behavior goal for the transition activity (and therefore fails to move one space on the board game), the motivation the next day is much improved. He has no problem getting the children to comply with the transition requests. Mr. Singh's class now is a model for how a second-grade class can behave during activity transitions.

WHAT IF?

- What might Mr. Singh do if transition to another activity became problematic?
- When should the Good Behavior Board Game be added to the high-p request sequences?
- How do you explain the effectiveness of the high-p request sequence in getting children to comply?

FORM

7.1 Transition Activity Charting Form—to be filled out by teacher.

FORM 7.1

Transition Activity Charting Form—to be filled out by teacher

Class: _____

Baseline or Intervention: _____

Date: _____   Period: _____   Transition Activity: _____

Student(s)	# of activity transition commands given	Commands followed (Yes/No)?

PART 3

Plans for Keeping on Task and Completing Assignments

Chapter 8

The Beeper System

Chapter 9

Task Engagement Program (TEP)

Chapter 10

Grandma's Rule for Increasing In-Seat Behavior

Chapter 11

Response Cards

INTRODUCTION

WHAT IS ON-TASK BEHAVIOR?

On-task behavior has been studied in many empirical investigations (Kazdin & Bootzin, 1972; Kazdin & Klock, 1973; Prater, Hogan, & Miller, 1992; Wolery, Bailey, & Sugai, 1988). It is commonly defined as the student attending to work or teacher-presented instruction. Specifically, in a paper-and-pencil task or a reading task, children are considered to be on task if they are engaged in either reading the materials ("face-to-book" orientation), or writing or looking at the paper. Examples of *off-task behavior* would involve students getting out of their seats, staring at the ceiling or floor, talking to a friend, and so on. In the case of teacher oral presentations, the child is expected to be looking in the teacher's direction. Therefore, any instances in which the child is not looking at the teacher are considered off task.

While measures of on-task behavior may not be ideal (from the standpoint of measuring a child's attention), they are acceptable approximations of a child's level of attention (Gunter, Venn, Patrick, Miller, & Kelly, 2003). Obviously, one cannot get inside the child's mind to see whether the information is being received and processed. It is possible that a child may be looking at the teacher but not attending and processing information. However, many studies have demonstrated a high correlation between attending (being on task) and work completion (Cohen & Close, 1975; Jackson, 1979; Schipp, Baker, & Cuvo, 1980).

WHAT CONSTITUTES ON-TASK AND ASSIGNMENT COMPLETION?

In many classes, on-task rates during class assignments or lectures vary from student to student. Some students are engaged in their assignments at a high level, others complete part of their work, and some children are infrequently engaged in their assignment (which produces minimal completion of their assignment).

Children who generate high levels of on-task behavior are generally those who complete the assignments. The converse is also generally true. Children who have performance problems are those who have low rates of work completion or high rates of inaccurate performance of the assignments, or both. They also demonstrate lower rates of on-task behavior.

When a child is capable of performing an assignment but does not perform the work accurately or on time because of a lack of motivation, a strategy to deal with this performance problem may be needed. The five management plans presented in part 3 of this text are well suited for these children. However, some children may also demonstrate performance problems that are the result of their lack of ability with the work (i.e., they do not understand the material). The management plans presented here would not address these children's needs (except the Response Cards instructional method); other teaching techniques would need to be considered.

THE RAMIFICATIONS OF ON-TASK AND ASSIGNMENT COMPLETION PROBLEMS

The long-term effects of a child's inability to stay on task and complete assignments can range from poor grades and low selfe-esteem to skill deficits in the academic content areas. Obviously, children who have adequate to good study habits profit more from the classroom learning environment than do students who have difficulty attending to teacher instruction or completing class or home assignments. Furthermore, children who are consistently off task often engage in disruptive behavior, which disturbs the learning environment for themselves and others.

DEALING WITH ON-TASK AND PERFORMANCE PROBLEMS

Teachers use several common strategies to deal with on-task problems and difficulty in completing assignments. In many cases, teachers will mildly admonish children who are not engaged in the reading or written assignments. For example, a child may start daydreaming and the teacher might comment, "Sarah, you need to get back to reading your assignment and not daydream so much." In many circumstances, the child attends to this directive (to engage in reading) at that point, and the teacher immediately attends to another child or task. However, this admonishment does not produce greater attention to the task in the long run for many children. Often, the teacher finds that children who have trouble remaining on task require more and more directives to stay engaged in the material.

A second strategy that has received empirical attention is to praise children when they are on task (Kazdin & Klock, 1973; Madsen, Becker, & Thomas, 1968; Walker, Hops, & Fiegenbaum, 1976). The teacher spots several children who are doing their work and draws attention to them in the following manner: "I like the way Bobby, Sharon, Rhonda, and Bill are doing their work. It is nice to see those students behaving well in class and learning the material." While praise has been shown to be effective in increasing on-task behavior, its use has to be extremely systematic and frequent to affect changes in children's on-task behavior. Very often the teacher monitors the class less frequently as time goes by, and subsequently the level of praise for such behavior goes down dramatically. With this infrequent attention to the children's on-task behavior, praise (by itself) becomes an ineffective strategy.

EFFECTIVE STRATEGIES FOR ON-TASK AND PERFORMANCE PROBLEMS

The behavioral plans presented in part 3 address two major requirements for increasing on-task behavior and accurate assignment completion: (a) the plan systematically provides for monitoring on-task behavior and subsequent reinforcing of this behavior when it does occur, and (b) the plan provides for the systematic monitoring of accurately completed assignments and reinforcement when the child completes class assignments.

In the case of the first requirement, several of the management strategies in this text require the teacher to monitor the students' behavior systematically to determine whether the children are on task. For example, in the Beeper System, the teacher is cued by a series of beeps to monitor on-task behavior across the entire class. Children who are on task at the time of the beeps are given points. The Task Engagement Program enables the teacher to monitor on-task behavior by noting when a student disengages from the task. In the case of Grandma's Rule, individual students are monitored as to their in-seat performance. Grandma's Rule invokes a contingency between staying in-seat for a relatively short time (low probability behavior) and getting out-of-seat (high probability behavior). Staying in-seat for a designated period of time results in the child being allowed to leave her seat. This can be an extremely effective tool for teaching young children to gradually learn how to stay in their seat and do their work.

A powerful way to increase student attending and on-task behavior involves creating more interesting instructional formats. Research has demonstrated that frequent opportunities to respond to questions affects the acquisition of skills and behavior during the instruction (Greenwood, Delquadri, & Hall, 1984). In the Response Card program (Narayan et al. 1990), the teacher presents a limited amount of information and then "tests" the children's comprehension using a dry erase board. Because each child will be asked to respond to questions frequently, attention and on-task behavior will increase (Armendariz & Umbreit, 1999; Gardner et al. 1994; Narayan et al. 1990).

The following list delineates the four management plans presented in this part and their application as relevant for individual student or class-wide applications.

Four Classroom Management Plans for Addressing On-Task Behavior		
Management Plan	**Individual**	**Classwide**
Beeper System	X	X
Task Engagement Program	X	X
Grandma's Rule	X	
Response Cards		X

8

The Beeper System

BRIEF DESCRIPTION

The beeper system is an excellent management strategy for monitoring student on-task behavior (Erken & Henderson, 1989; Repp, Barton, & Brulle, 1983). The system uses a momentary time sampling method (Gunter, Venn, Patrick, Miller, & Kelly, 2003) during one or more class periods with the generation of random signals or beeps. The signal or beep cues the teacher to scan the classroom and identify who is on task and who is off task (Erken & Henderson, 1989; Henderson, Jenson, Erken, Davidsmeyer, & Lampe, 1986). Points are awarded to those students identified by the teacher as being on task at the time of the signal or beep. In some cases, students may be trained to accurately monitor their own behavior and record points if they were on task.

At the end of the assignment or period, the number of points each student has earned is summed. Those students achieving or exceeding the behavior standard (usually set as a number of total earned points) trade in their points for a desired reinforcer. What they get and how much they get can be a function of how many points they earned that period. For example, students earning 80% of the total points could get 3 minutes of extra recess, whereas students who earn 95% of the total points would earn 5 extra minutes. A master chart keeps track of each child's points each time the beeper system is used. Self-monitoring children keep their own charts.

The beeper system provides random but frequent signals or beeps in the beginning stage of implementation to increase the chances of catching the children on task. The number of beeps is gradually reduced as the children need less frequent monitoring to stay on task. The beeper system can be used for one or a few children who have extremely low rates of on-task behavior as well as for an entire class.

TERMS

behavior standard the number of points a child must earn to access reinforcement.

self-monitor students determine individually if they are on task at each beep and record the designated number of points earned.

APPARATUS

A preferable piece of apparatus is a 3-ounce electronic device (it looks like a pager) called the MotivAider.[1] This device can be programmed to produce a pulsing vibration signal at varying intervals. Only the person wearing the device is aware of the signal. This allows the teacher more time to observe each student without "tipping him off." The vibration signal can be adjusted in strength and duration at the teacher's discretion. It has time control keys that allow you to set the average interval length, as well as a user key that can program either fixed or variable intervals. Upon the vibration signal being

---

[1] The Motiv-Aider, invented by Dr. Steve Levinson, is available through Behavioral Dynamics, located in Thief River Falls, MN. Further information can be found at www.habitchange.com.

delivered, the teacher can scan the class unobtrusively to monitor on-task behavior of the target students or entire class. The teacher can provide oral feedback as to the on-task behavior of each student on the student point chart. To ensure that the students do not anticipate the teacher's scanning at fixed intervals, periodically delay the feedback 10–30 seconds after the signal. This is more necessary with average interval lengths of 2, 3, or 4 minutes.

An audiotape with a series of beeps occurring at variable intervals can be used if the MotivAider is not available. It is difficult to make the audiotape beep unobtrusive. A set of audiotapes can be purchased.[2] Each tape produces 1-second beeps for a designated period of time. Let's say the teacher uses the beeper system for a 45-minute class period. She wishes to start with 30 beeps within that time frame. She would purchase or develop several 45-minute audiotapes, with the time sequence of beeps different for each tape. Obviously, if only a single tape was used, students would quickly learn the pattern of beeps for that tape (and then learn to go on task selectively!). If 6 to 9 tapes are developed, students would be hard pressed to memorize the patterns on all the tapes.

If the MotivAider or audiotapes are not available, an oven timer can be used. The teacher designates a time interval in which the timer is to be set (e.g., between 10 and 40 seconds). The teacher sets the timer for a value between those 2 points (e.g., 10 and 40 seconds). When the timer goes off, the teacher scans the class for on-task behavior, notes who gets points, and then resets the timer for a value within those 2 points again. The process of setting the oven timer is repeated until the end of the period. I strongly recommend the use of the MotivAider, because it enables the teacher to scan the students or entire class without the students recognizing that monitoring of on-task behavior is occurring.

Another necessary item is the Student Point Chart, which records the points each student has earned on the beeper system. Figure 8.1 is a sample student point chart that illustrates a 7-beep system for a 20-minute period for 3 students. The maximum number of points possible is 35. The number of points needed to earn 3 and 5 minutes of extra free time is 26 and 32 points, respectively.

Time frame: <u>20 minutes</u>
Number of beeps: <u>7</u>
Total possible points: <u>35</u>
Total points needed for 3 minutes free time: <u>26</u>
Total points needed for 5 minutes free time: <u>32</u>

Student/Beep	1	2	3	4	5	6	7	Total Points
J. L.	3	0	6	2	5	10	5	31
R. V.	3	4	0	2	0	0	5	14
S. T.	3	4	6	2	0	10	5	30

FIGURE 8.1
A Sample Student Point Chart: Beeper System

[2] The Erken Learning Center, 1904 Marin Drive, Santa Rosa, CA 95405

| (total possible points: 100) | | | | | |
Variation/Number of Beeps	1	2	3	4	5
A	27	13	31	19	10
B	12	31	23	18	16
C	6	30	27	25	12
D	15	4	15	2	14
E	20	5	9	12	4

FIGURE 8.2
A Sample Beeper Point Card

The point total for each student across the 20-minute period is given in the right-hand column. The chart shows that J. L. and S. T. earned 3 minutes of extra free time (by earning 31 and 30 points, respectively). R. V., who earned only 14 points total, did not earn free time.

Finally, a beeper "point card" with point values should be made. When implementing the beeper system, it is wise to not provide the same number of points for each beep (otherwise students learn that if they have reached the standard early, they can coast for the rest of the period). The teacher should use a variety of point payoffs at each beep. The beeper card provides 5 to 7 variations of points across the number of beeps, so the students never know which beeps produce large numbers of points. Figure 8.2 shows a sample beeper point card presenting 5 variations of a 5-beep system. Note that in Variation A a 10-point payoff occurs on the fifth beep. One would not want the students to learn that the fifth beep on the tape always results in 10 points. Sometimes, it results in 4 points (Variation E).

BASELINE MEASUREMENT

Baseline measurement involves determining the frequency of a behavior before a systematic technique is introduced. Its primary function is to enable the teacher to determine a reasonable behavior standard to use in the initial implementation of the plan. A reasonable standard is neither too high nor too low. For example, if a child is on task 40–60% of the time, a behavior standard of 90% would be too high. Conversely, a behavior standard of 20% is probably too easy. A reasonable standard would be between 40% and 60%.

A baseline measurement of on-task behavior for this system merely requires the teacher to implement the beeper system in a designated class period without specifying the standard or providing the ability to earn special reinforcers. The teacher monitors on-task behavior during each vibrating signal or beep (depending on which system is being used) and assigns points to the students who are on task. If desired, the teacher can let the students know how many points they have earned at the end of the period, as a partial incentive to remain on task. However, no reinforcers are available during the baseline measurement.

After collecting baseline measurements for 5 to 8 days, the teacher is able to establish the number of points the students must get to earn the reinforcer. This is done by examining the baseline data across all students and arriving at a reasonable standard. In some cases, only a single standard will be set (e.g., 80% of the total points). If there are several low performers in the class who might not reach this standard, 2 or more standards can be set in a graded fashion (e.g., 60% of the total points earns 2 minutes, 80% earns 4 minutes).

PROCEDURES

1. Purchase the MotivAider (preferable), beeper tapes, or an oven timer (see the Apparatus section earlier in this chapter).

2. Designate class period(s) in which the beeper system will be used and the subsequent time frame (e.g., 40 minutes or 50 minutes).

3. Design a student point chart (see Form 8.1 or Form 8.2 for groups and a beeper point card (see Form 8.3). Specify the number of beeps to occur on the point chart. Design several points variations for the sequence of beeps.

4. Collect baseline data using a beeper system for 5 to 8 days, but do not provide a special reinforcer for getting points nor set a standard during baseline monitoring. Begin using a variable interval of 3 minutes for young children and slightly more for older students as the baseline monitoring system.

5. After collecting baseline data, calculate the number of points the students will need across the class period to achieve the standard. If necessary, a graded system of 2 or more standards can be used (e.g., 80% of the total points produces 4 minutes of free time, and 90% produces 8 minutes of free time).

6. Inform the class of the beeper system.

7. Implement the beeper system during one target class period initially and appoint a chart manager for each period (see Additional Considerations in the following text) to record each student's points for each beep during the class period.

8. When the vibrating signal occurs (or the beep goes off if using audiotapes), scan the class, call out those students who earn points (or if only a few are off task, call off those who do not earn points). Provide intermittent praise for on-task behavior in addition to point allocation.

9. After the points are distributed, continue teaching.

10. Repeat the process with each beep and at the end of the period total up the number of points for each student. Determine who reached the behavior standard needed for free time (or whatever reinforcement is being used) and deliver the reinforcement.

HOW IT WORKS

The beeper system enables the teacher to track on-task behavior without substantially disrupting the instructional system. With continued practice, most teachers who have used this system report eventually becoming comfortable with the system, particularly as the number of beeps is reduced.

Additionally, if the teacher is using the MotivAider, she or he can learn to scan faster with practice across several days or weeks, because the signal is prominent only to the teacher and is unobtrusive to the students.

With frequent, unpredictable monitoring and with feedback to students as to whether they are on task, student on-task behavior increases. As a result of the setting of the standard and the availability of a reinforcer for achieving the standard, students become more motivated to stay on task and earn the reinforcer.

ADDITIONAL CONSIDERATIONS

Appointing a Chart Manager

If the beeper system is implemented by the teacher, it is advisable for the teacher to appoint a chart manager from the class for each period. By delegating the function of record-keeping, the teacher can proceed with instruction after scanning the class and assigning the points to students who are on task. The chart manager records this data, then returns to the assignment. The chart manager should be a different student each period so that no one person is allowed to perform this duty every day. A different student can be selected each period as a special treat.

Keeping Up with the Beeper System

The beeper system, as well as other behavior programs, has inherent logistical issues in its implementation. The beeper system requires the frequent scanning of students, quick decisions about each student's current engagement with a task (if conducted across whole class) and the recording of points. With practice, a teacher can dramatically improve his or her ability to scan, evaluate, and record points, in contrast to the first day of implementation. Again, the use of the MotivAider as the mechanism to signal the teacher to scan the classroom would make it easier to perform the requirements of the beeper system, particularly in the beginning.

Monitoring Performance in Groups

In some classes, the individual monitoring of each student may prove difficult. The teacher might consider the use of the beeper system in monitoring the on-task behavior of several groups of students, as exemplified in the Henderson et al. (1986) study (see chapter 1). While this method still requires the teacher to scan the entire class at each beep, the recording of on-task behavior is performed in groups.

To accomplish this form of monitoring, it is advisable to have a seating arrangement that clusters the students into the small groups. When the beep or signal occurs, scan each group. All students in the respective group must be on task for the entire group to earn points. If any student is not on task at the signal, no one in the group earns points for that beep. The data sheet for the group monitoring system is presented in Form 8.2.

Teaching Students to Self-Monitor

At some point teachers should consider having students monitor their own on-task behavior and record the points they have earned, with teacher spot-checks for accurate monitoring (McLaughlin, 1983, 1984). The specifics of a self-monitoring program are the same as for one using a chart manager, except that each student has a separate recording sheet (see Form 8.1). With each beep, the students identify whether they are on task and write down the number of points stated by the teacher. If the teacher is using the MotivAider, she or he would call out the self-check with each vibrating signal. At the end, the points are totaled and reinforcement is delivered to students reaching the standard. To ensure student accuracy, the teacher can conduct random spot checks of the recording sheets.

The stipulation to conduct spot checks on student's recordings has been found in research to be important for improving the accuracy of some student's self-observation during self-monitoring (Bolstad & Johnson, 1972). While many students will be accurate without spot checking, a teacher may not be able to discern a priori which student(s) will be an accurate observer of on-task behavior. To ensure that student self-observation matches what the teacher would record as being on task, a random spot-check procedure covering all students who are self-monitoring is highly recommended.

Low Performers

In some cases, low performers may not achieve the standard necessary for reinforcement. In this case, a lower behavior standard might be deployed for those students. Consider the following hypothetical data recorded over an 8-day period (percentage of total points earned) as a case of selecting an alternate standard for initial low performers:

> J. F. earned 80% or more of the total points on only 1 day and more than 60% on 5 days. Therefore, 60% might be selected as an initial standard for J. F. As J. F. achieves this standard regularly (8 out of 10 days), the standard is increased (e.g., 70%).

Another adaptation for low performers is to reduce the length of the time they are on the beeper system. For example, a 45-minute period for the class on the beeper system might be shortened for the low performers to the first 25 minutes. The low performers would not use the system for the remaining 20 minutes. Again, as they become adept at remaining on task, the length of time they are on the beeper system is increased.

Finally, the number of beeps might be increased to enable the teacher more of an opportunity to catch the low-performing children on task. Therefore, low performers might be on a separate tape (with different intervals between beeps) from the rest of the class, to allow for a greater number of beeps.

Increasing the Behavior Standard

Particularly when a standard has been set lower than the desirable goal for on-task behavior, the teacher should consider progressively increasing the standard. This is done with the aid of data.

For example, after 2 weeks of implementing the beeper system, the teacher may find that all students in the class have achieved the behavior standard of 65 (out of 100 points) on 8 of the 10 days in which the beeper system was implemented for a class period. She might then increase the behavior standard to 70 points needed to earn the reinforcement. If in the next 2 to 3 weeks, students reliably achieve or exceed this level, the teacher can again increase the standard by a few points (e.g., to 73). This process continues until the teacher is satisfied with the standard of on-task behavior and the students are able to reliably achieve or exceed the standard.

Gradually Reducing the "Density" of Beeps

In the initial implementation of the beeper system, the density of the signals or beeps is great, so that the teacher can catch the children on task more frequently. Once the children begin responding to the system with increased on-task levels, the teacher can gradually and systematically reduce the number of beeps (see Form 8.4). The following suggested density of signals or beeps occurring over multiple phases could be adapted by the teacher for a 1-hour instructional period. Phase I encumbers the baseline and initial implementation.

Phase I signal about every 3 minutes

Phase II signal about every 6 minutes

Phase III signal about every 9 minutes

Phase IV signal about every 12 minutes

Phase V signal about every 15 minutes

Phase VI signal about every 20 minutes

With this progressive reduction of signals, the teacher would begin at Phase I (or Phase II for some classes). She would implement the next phase once the students increased their on-task behavior to a desirable level. If this level is maintained for 2 to 3 weeks, the teacher goes to the next phase. This progressive reduction continues, contingent on student performance remaining at high levels, until the teacher reaches Phase V or VI.

A "Graded" System for Earning Reinforcement

In some cases, it might be wise to have 2 sets of behavior standards, high and low. The high standard, such as 90 points out of 100, might provide 5 minutes of extra video time on Friday. However, to ensure that students don't give up once they have figured out they can't possibly get 90 points (after being off task for a couple of beeps), a low standard might be set at 75 points, enabling students to earn 2 minutes of extra video time.

By using such a graded system, you can keep the students motivated, even during sessions in which they have a couple of instances of off-task behavior.

HYPOTHETICAL EXAMPLE: TWO LOW-PERFORMING TARGET STUDENTS

Mr. Johanson is considering using the beeper system for 2 students in his sixth-grade class who have unacceptable levels of on-task behavior. He estimates that their on-task behavior on some days is less than 20%. He purchases the MotivAider and decides to use the beeper system during the 9–10 A.M. class period. He divides the 50-minute period into two 20-minute periods (with a 10-minute break in between). He wants to have 10 signals occur during each 20-minute period, meaning the vibrating signal will be sent to him about every 2 minutes on average.

To determine the initial behavior standard, he collects baseline data on the 2 students for 5 days. He establishes a 50-point maximum possible number of points for a 20-minute period. The baseline data indicate that Student A ranges from a low of 5 points to a high of 25 points, with a mean of 16. Student B has a low of 5 and a high of 30, with a mean of 20. Mr. Johanson decides to set a single standard for both students because they are fairly similar in their average rate of on-task behavior. The behavior standard is the following: If the students earn 15 points, they get 5 minutes of an alternate preferred activity at the end of the 20-minute time frame. If they earn 20 points, they get 10 minutes of an alternate activity after the 20-minute time frame. If they do not earn either 5 or 10-minutes, they will continue working until the next time frame. Therefore, the students may work for 20 minutes and then have a 10-minute alternate in-seat activity period before working for another 20 minutes, followed by another 10 minutes of alternate activity (if they earn the maximum possible).

Mr. Johanson informs the students of the beeper system, how it works, and how many points they have to accumulate in the 20-minute period to earn 5 or 10 minutes of an alternate activity. He posts a form with the specific details (see Form 8.5). He sets the beeper point card in the top drawer of his desk, sets the MotivAider to a variable 2-minute signal, places it in his pocket, and implements the system. When he receives the signal, he immediately observes the 2 target students and records the points each has earned. He continues teaching, working with students who need help. At the end of the 20-minute period when all the 10 signals have occurred and points have been recorded, he determines immediately which of the students (or both) has earned an alternate activity. The student who has earned 10 minutes can stop at that point and engage in an alternate in-seat activity. If the student earned only 5 minutes, she or he must continue working 5 more minutes before engaging in the more preferred alternate activity. If the students do not earn any alternate activity time, they must continue working for the entire 10-minute time period before the next 20-minute work period.

After 2 weeks of implementation, Mr. Johanson is pleased with the results. Both students have done so well that the behavior standard is now 35 out of 50 points to earn 5 minutes of free time and 45 points to earn

10 minutes. Both students have earned at least 5 minutes of free time at every opportunity in the past several days.

HYPOTHETICAL EXAMPLE: HIGH SCHOOL AMERICAN HISTORY

Mrs. Chang loves to teach high school American history. While some students in her third-period class are engaged and ask pertinent questions during the lecture, others use the time to send text messages to their friends when she is not looking. Mrs. Chang purchases the MotivAider and places students in 3 groups of 8, 9, and 9 students. The groups are named after the capitals of 2 neighboring states and of course their state, Georgia. The groups are Tallahassee, Birmingham, and Atlanta. She collects baseline data for 2 weeks by recording whether every member of the group was on task during the inaudible signal given off by the MotivAider. The MotivAider is set for a variable interval of 3 minutes across the 45 minutes in the third period. The summary data for points earned across the 3 groups for the 11 baseline sessions is presented in a table (100 points possible).

Day/Group	Tallahassee	Birmingham	Atlanta
1	43	40	32
2	39	45	38
3	50	47	45
4	57	58	46
5	46	55	60
6	67	49	68
7	55	38	70
8	56	50	65
9	49	67	55
10	39	39	35
11	60	60	55
Average (mean)	51	46	52

Mrs. Chang decides to use the same behavior standard for all 3 groups because their average point score is similar. She selects a graded system for all groups: 50 points earns 5 stars and 60 points earns 10 stars. At the end of the week (Thursday class), any group that has earned at least 25 stars can have the following week free from homework and also will be excused from the last 10 minutes of the class. Any group failing to earn 25 points will have to stay the entire class and have their homework assignments letter graded.

On the first day of implementation, Mrs. Chang observes the members of each group when she feels the MotivAider vibrate, being careful not to tip off anyone that she is making a recording until she has scanned every group. The first day results in the following point totals for each group: Tallahassee 66, Birmingham 66, and Atlanta 58. Both the Tallahassee and Birmingham groups earned enough points to gain 10 stars toward the week's total. Atlanta earned 5 stars. Mrs. Chang sees that this system will make it easier for the students to pay attention, and she is ready to continue its use.

WHAT IF?

- What should Mrs. Chang do if any of the students failed to earn any preferred time for the first 2 weeks of the plan in the first example?

- What data might indicate that the number of signals or beeps is too infrequent for one or both students in the first example? What would be the solution?

- What steps could Mr. Johanson take so that the beeper system could eventually be run across a 40-minute period during the 9–10 A.M. class period, with just a 10-minute alternate activity reinforcer?

- What if a teacher found it hard to record points? Could a different system be used? What might be put in place to have students record their points?

- What are some considerations in using the group monitoring method in the second example?

FORMS

8.1 Student Self-Management Chart: 20 Beeps (or Signals)

8.2 Group Monitoring Chart: 20 Beeps (or Signals), Five Groups

8.3 Beeper Card

8.4 Beeper System: Teacher-Designated Plan—Teacher uses this form for written plan.

8.5 Beeper System: Class Posting of Rules—Teacher posts this form for students to view.

FORM 8.1

Student Self-Management Chart: 20 Beeps (or Signals)

Student's Name _____

Date _____ Period _____

Total possible points _____ Number of points needed _____

<u>Beeps</u>   <u>Points awarded</u>

1

2

3

4

5

6

7

8

9

10

11

12

13

14

15

16

17

18

19

20

Total

FORM 8.2

Group Monitoring Chart: 20 Beeps (or Signals), Five Groups

Signal/Group	Group A	Group B	Group C	Group D	Group E
1					
2					
3					
4					
5					
6					
7					
8					
9					
10					
11					
12					
13					
14					
15					
16					
17					
18					
19					
20					

───────── **FORM 8.3** ─────────

Beeper Card

100 points possible—four variations of points across 10 beeps

	Number of Beeps									
	1	2	3	4	5	6	7	8	9	10
Variation A	5	15	6	9	21	7	2	18	12	5
Variation B	9	6	21	15	5	12	5	7	2	18
Variation C	13	13	5	14	8	7	1	19	12	8
Variation D	7	12	9	8	20	24	3	9	4	4

―――――――――― **FORM 8.4** ――――――――――

Beeper System: Teacher-Designated Plan

Target class:

On-task behavior(s):

Baseline data across students in class for five sessions (average percentage of on-task behavior across all students):

     (1) _____

     (2) _____

     (3) _____

     (4) _____

     (5) _____

Standard for earning reinforcement (number of points needed):

Criteria for adjusting standard up: _____

Criteria for adjusting standard down: _____

Number of initial signals or beeps: _____

Criteria for decreasing number of signals or beeps: _____

Parental consent (if needed): _____

Administrator signature (if needed): _____

FORM 8.5

Beeper System: Class Posting of Rules

Rule: Remain in your seat and engaged in your work.

Total number of points possible: _____

Number of points needed: _____

Class periods/time for beeper system: _____

9

Task Engagement Program (TEP)

BRIEF DESCRIPTION

The Task Engagement Program (TEP) may be well suited for classrooms where the Beeper System is not feasible. One of the logistical difficulties with the Beeper System is the requirement to scan the target students when the signal or beep occurs and record whether each child is on task. This obviously becomes more difficult with larger classes, particularly if one is not using the MotivAider with an unobtrusive signal. With large classes, if one uses an audiotape, students may hear the beep and quickly initiate task engagement before being observed off task. The TEP does not require the teacher to scan an entire class at the end of a given interval. Rather, the teacher immediately notes when a given student is not engaged in the assignment and marks the entire interval as one of disengagement for that particular student (Kaufman & O'Leary, 1972). This makes it much easier to use this plan. Like the Beeper System, the TEP focuses on student engagement with the task or attention to teacher-directed instruction.

The teacher delineates a series of equal intervals in the target period(s). For example, a 1-hour instructional period can be divided into 4 15-minute intervals or time segments. In each interval, if the student demonstrates "task engagement" behavior, she or he earns a star for that interval. The behavioral requirement for earning a star in a given interval is to engage in the task or attend to the instruction for the entire interval. When the student does not demonstrate task engagement behavior for any part of that interval, the teacher records a 0 for that interval. Each new interval reinstitutes the behavioral requirement. If the student earns a preset number of stars over the target period(s) for the day, called the behavior standard, she or he earns access to a preferred activity that day.

It is essential that the teacher defines *task disengagement* in order for the TEP to be implemented effectively. For example, seat-work assignments require that the student attend to the instructional material and answer questions regarding the material. Any behavior that interferes with this activity is called disengagement and results in the failure to earn a star for that interval.

The TEP can be used for one or a few children who have extremely low rates of on-task behavior and assignment completions. It can also be used easily for an entire class, because the teacher does not have to scan the class at the end of the interval. Any children who disengage during the interval are scored as such at that point when their disengagement became conspicuous to the teacher. All students who were not observed to disengage within the interval receive stars at the end of the interval. Recording the stars for each student who earned them can be done by a "star chart" manager.

TERMS

task engagement student is engaged in the instructional materials or attending to the teacher's presentation for the length of the interval. Task engagement for independent seat work would entail attending to the instructional material, reading, and/or writing. Task engagement during a teacher's lecture is attending to the teacher's presentation, usually facing the teacher while she or he lectures or facing the paper while taking notes.

whole interval recording the TEP practice of awarding points to a student only if she or he works throughout the entire interval, for example, 20 minutes.

disengagement the display of a behavior(s) that breaks task engagement for a period of time (the length of time that is considered unacceptable is subjectively determined by the teacher).

behavioral standard the number of stars a student must earn to receive reinforcement.

preferred activities time (PAT) a period of time during which students who have earned PAT can engage in preferred activities (Jones, 1987).

APPARATUS

This program requires the use of an oven timer or some other timing mechanism that can be reset for each new interval. An audio signal should be produced at the end of the interval so that the recording of task engagement occurs and the teacher begins the next interval for the instructional period.

Additionally, a Task Engagement Card needs to be created if the program is to be used for a few select students (see Form 9.1). If the teacher is implementing TEP across the entire class, a Task Engagement Chart needs to be made to keep track of the number of stars each student needs and how many stars are earned (see Form 9.2). This chart delineates each student's name, the number of intervals comprising the target period, and the specification of a star or zero for each interval of that period.

BASELINE MEASUREMENT

As delineated in the Beeper System, baseline measurement involves determining the level of a behavior before a systematic technique is introduced. The primary function of the baseline measurement in the TEP is to enable the teacher to determine a reasonable behavior standard to use for each student in the beginning of this program.

Baseline measurement of task engagement merely requires the teacher to implement the TEP in the target class period(s) without specifying the behavioral standard for each child or providing the preferred activities for achieving a certain level of points. The teacher merely indicates to each child how many stars she or he earned and coaxes the child to try just as hard or harder tomorrow. As in the beeper system, feedback regarding their performance is used only during baseline.

Once 5 to 8 days of baseline data are collected, the teacher is able to establish the number of stars each student needs in order to earn preferred activities time that day (see Appendix A for ideas and suggestions on powerful reinforcers). While the teacher could certainly set a single standard for all students, the TEP is well suited to establishing a reasonable behavioral standard for each student individually. In that manner, students would "compete" against themselves, needing only to improve upon their baseline level of performance to earn preferred activities. For some children, the behavioral standard might be only enough stars for the student to be credited with 50% of the intervals as having earned a star. With some other students, it may be set at 75% of the intervals. The teacher can select a reasonable behavioral standard for each child as a function of baseline data.

PROCEDURES

1. Designate the target class period(s) that the TEP will be used.

2. Designate the equal interval lengths, for example, 15-minute intervals across a 1-hour math period, or 10-minute intervals across a 40-minute language arts period.

3. Calculate the total possible number of stars that can be earned in the target period.

4. Determine whether this program will be in effect for one to several students or the entire class and design the appropriate charting system for points (see Forms 9.1, 9.2, and 9.3).

5. Inform student(s) of the charting system and the scoring of task engagement in an interval as a function of their behavior (e.g., "You receive a star at the end of the interval for working hard on the assignment or attending to me when I am talking during each interval").

6. Designate what behaviors would be examples of disengagement, such as, getting out of seat, and place these behaviors on a chart for students to view.

7. Collect baseline data using the TEP charting system, providing feedback on the number of stars each student has earned and encouraging each student to improve the next day.

8. After collecting baseline data, calculate the behavioral standard for each individual student during the target period.

9. Initiate the TEP by informing each student of their target number of stars needed to earn reinforcement and the rules posted in plain view in the classroom (see Form 9.4).

10. Whenever a student disengages from the task or oral instruction for a certain period of time (beyond just a reasonable "stretch break"), record a zero for that interval right away and inform the student immediately of his or her disengagement.

11. For each student who did not receive a zero in the interval, when the interval elapses, award a star for that interval, reset the timer for a new interval, and repeat the process.

12. Continue teaching or managing instruction subsequently. For classwide implementation, a teacher may want to appoint a star chart manager, similar to the one described in the beeper system.

13. At the end of the class, determine which students reached their behavioral standard and provide preferred activities time at the arranged time.

14. For those who do not earn PAT, they can work on a new or previous assignment during others' PAT.

HOW IT WORKS

The TEP requires the teacher to record disengagement from the task or instruction at the point at which it is observed. It does not require the teacher to make simultaneous judgments about task engagement of many students within a short few seconds. Anyone who was not spotted as being disengaged during that preceding interval is awarded a star. While the TEP may not "catch" minor instances of disengagement, a vigilant teacher should be able to monitor many students for their attention to the task or teacher presentation.

As a result of setting individual behavioral standards, the reinforcement plan is tailored initially to fit each student's ability. With the opportunity to earn preferred activities, students will strive to reach their goal and receive feedback every interval in terms of their progress. Once the individual student is reliably achieving his or her target behavioral standard, a more stringent target can be set. In this manner, students who start with relatively low star totals can be "shaped" toward higher levels of task engagement.

ADDITIONAL CONSIDERATIONS

Appointing a Star Chart Manager

As in the beeper system, the TEP entails data collection. If more than several students will be in the program, it is advisable for the teacher to appoint a star chart manager from the class for each period. Again, my advice is to appoint a different student each period as a "treat."

Teaching Students to Self-Monitor

Self-monitoring can be deployed with this program with the same caveats as mentioned in the self-monitoring component of the Beeper System. Each student in this program has a separate recording sheet (see Form 9.1). With the elapse of each interval, the students decide whether they demonstrated task engagement throughout the interval and enter a "yes" in either the column marked "star" on Form 9.1 or the column marked "zero."

This program will require a bit more teaching of the criteria for self-monitoring than the beeper system. In the Beeper System detailed in chapter 8, the student evaluates whether she or he was on task at the beep. In this program, the student must evaluate whether she or he disengaged from the instruction or task at any point during the interval. Obviously, this is a more subjective judgment than what is required in the Beeper System. The teacher should strongly consider a 2-week grace period for self-monitoring. In this period, discrepancies between the student's evaluation of his or her task engagement and the teacher's evaluation (via random spot checks of the student's recording sheets) are merely pointed out. No additional consequence beyond losing the disputed star is taken. After the grace period, an additional fine is levied for such disagreements.

Notes

Shaping Task Engagement

If the percentage of intervals that result in a star during the baseline is extremely low, it may be necessary to adjust the interval to a smaller time frame. For example, if a student usually scored only 1 or 2 stars out of 10 possible intervals (20-minute interval lengths), it might be useful to reduce the interval to 10 minutes and collect more baseline data with that new interval length. If the student scores 10 or more stars out of 20 intervals in the following days, reducing the interval length seems to be the "fix." It might be necessary with some students to adjust the interval length to 5 minutes, making 12 intervals in a 60-minute period. This will give the teacher more opportunity to "catch them being good," particularly for students who disengage from the instruction at higher rates.

In other cases, the number of behaviors that define disengagement might be a few in the beginning of the program. For example, disengagement might initially be defined as getting out of one's seat or verbally disturbing other students. Once the student can handle this requirement (as seen by his or her earning a high percentage of stars), an additional requirement can be added, such as looking away from the task materials for longer than a 15-second period, even if not disturbing anyone.

Another adaptation for the TEP can be the allowance of one warning to reengage in the task per interval. Consider using a warning system if the target student has a low rate of achieving stars across the vast majority of intervals. If the student fails to achieve the behavioral standard for 6 to 8 consecutive days, consider providing a warning before recording a 0 for any given interval. Once the child begins earning stars reliably with a warning system, then you can return to the TEP as originally described.

Increasing the Behavioral Standard

The changing of the behavioral standard is done for each individual student, because the TEP sets an individualized behavioral standard for each student. For example, after 4 weeks of implementing the TEP, Raul has earned the daily reinforcer 19 out of 20 times, with the behavioral standard set at 60% of intervals having stars. The teacher might then increase the behavior standard to 70% stars to earn the daily reinforcement. If in the next 4 weeks Raul reliably achieves or exceeds this level, the behavioral standard can be increased again. This progressive alteration of the behavioral standard is continued until an acceptable level of performance is achieved.

A "Graded" System for Earning Reinforcement

As in the case of the Beeper System, it might be wise to have 2 sets of behavioral standards, high and low. By using such a graded system, you can keep most students motivated even during sessions in which they have not earned stars for several intervals. For example, earning 60–75% of the total possible stars results in 5 minutes of PAT, whereas 75% or above results in 12 minutes of PAT.

HYPOTHETICAL EXAMPLE: CLASSWIDE IMPLEMENTATION OF THE TEP

Ms. Rinaldo feels that her entire class of fourth-grade students could benefit from the TEP during math in-seat work. She realizes that practicing multiple digit addition and subtraction problems, as well as multiplication and division problems, is not the most exciting activity on the planet. However, the value of becoming more adept, that is, accurate and fluent, with calculation problems requires a certain amount of practice.

She divides the 40-minute drill period into 4 10-minute periods. The oven timer will be set every 10 minutes. To determine the initial behavioral standard for each student, she collects baseline data for 10 days. The students were apprised of the requirement to do their work and not bother other students or engage in doodling or other reading (definition of disengagement) when the oven timer is set for this period. During each math period, she indicated to the students how many stars they earned.

Every student had at least 1 day in which she or he earned all 4 stars. Most students earned 3 stars a period. Only 2 students had the majority of the baseline days, having earned just 2 stars (P. T. and R. V.). With these data, Ms. Rinaldo explains the program to the students again, indicating that if they meet their personal goal, each student can have 10 minutes of drawing, doodling, or conversation time right after the lunch recess and before California history period. Students who do not meet their personal goal would have additional practice on the math drill sheets during that time in a corner of the room supervised by Ms. Rinaldo. All the students except P. T. and R. V. are required to earn at least 3 stars to earn the 10-minute preferred activities time. P. T. and R. V. must earn at least 2 stars.

After 4 weeks of implementation, all students regularly achieved their daily personal goal. Furthermore, 22 out of the 25 students with a 3-star requirement never had a day when they earned fewer than 3 stars (quite an improvement over baseline). Both P. T. and R. V. have done well, earning enough stars every single day. Ms. Rinaldo moves their personal goal to 3 stars, making their requirement now as stringent as the other students in the class. Ms. Rinaldo tells both students that their performance has improved over the last 4 weeks and that they can handle it. They agree!

WHAT IF?

- How would you decide when to alter the interval length? What data might indicate that the interval length should be shortened?
- When should the student be allowed to self-monitor?
- What might be done to make it easier for the teacher to be aware of the students' behavior? How difficult might it be to use the TEP across larger classes?
- What are the advantages of the TEP over the Beeper System? Do you prefer the TEP or the beeper system using the MotivAider? Why? Is the beeper system better in accuracy of measurement? Why?

Notes

Notes

FORMS

9.1 Task Engagement Program Card: Individual Student—Six intervals.

9.2 Task Engagement Program Chart—Entire Class—Teacher uses this form for specific program for tracking a number of individual students.

9.3 TEP: Teacher-Designated Plan—Teacher uses this form for written plan.

9.4 TEP: Class Posting of Rules—Teacher posts this for students to view.

FORM 9.1

Task Engagement Program Card: Individual Student—Six Intervals

Student's name: _____

Length of interval: _____ (six intervals)

Date: _____ Period: _____

Total possible stars: 6   Number needed: _____

Interval	Stars	Zero
1		
2		
3		
4		
5		
6		

— FORM 9.2 —

Task Engagement Program Chart—Entire Class

Class: _____

Length of interval: _____

Number of intervals: _____

Date: _____ Period: _____

Total possible stars: _____

<u>Student</u>   <u>Number of stars needed</u>   <u>Number earned</u>

─────── **FORM 9.3** ───────

TEP: Teacher-Designated Plan

Target student(s):

Disengagement behaviors:

Length of interval:

Baseline data across five students (average number of stars earned across each student):

Student	Average number of stars	Behavioral standard
1.	1.	1.
2.	2.	2.
3.	3.	3.
4.	4.	4.
5.	5.	5.

Criteria for adjusting behavioral standard up: _____

Criteria for adjusting behavioral standard down: _____

Parental consent (if needed): _____

Administrator's signature (If Needed): _____

FORM 9.4

TEP: Class Posting of Rules

Interval length:

Rule: Remain in your seat and engaged in your work for entire interval to get a star.

Total number of stars possible: _____

Grandma's Rule for Increasing In-Seat Behavior

BRIEF DESCRIPTION

Some children, especially younger children, have difficulty remaining in their seat for relatively long periods. In early elementary grades, some classroom activities require the child to sit for 10, 20, or even 30 minutes. Children who have the ability to sit for only a few minutes at a time obviously would have difficulty with these activities. Teachers report that many children have difficulty sitting (and attending) for a period of time, even after being referred for medication, counseling, and so on.

The management plan presented in this chapter gradually increases in-seat behavior using a principle inherent in Grandma's Rule (Premack, 1959, 1965). Grandma's Rule goes something like this: "You don't get your dessert until you eat your vegetables." The rule describes a basic relationship between an undesirable event (eating vegetables) and a preferred event (eating dessert). This basic relationship between undesirable events and preferred events can be used to increase desirable behaviors (Hopkins, Schutte, & Garton, 1971; Kern, Mantegna, Vorndran, Bailin, & Hilt, 2001). The teacher would require the child to be in-seat for a short designated period of time. If the child stays in-seat for this time period, the teacher would allow the child to get out of his seat for some period of time. In other words, the child would earn out-of-seat time (more probable event) for being in-seat (less probable event) for a certain amount of time.

To use Grandma's Rule to increase in-seat behavior, the teacher identifies the child's current ability to remain in-seat. He collects baseline data on the rate of out-of-seat occurrences during a designated class period. If the child gets out of his seat 5 times in a 20-minute period, the average interval of in-seat behavior can be computed (see Form 10.1). The teacher divides the number of times the child gets out of his seat (5) into the length of the period (20). This would yield the *average* interval of in-seat behavior. (In this case, the average interval would be 4 minutes.)

With this average interval of in-seat behavior identified, a behavior standard is set. Usually the teacher can use this average length, or something close to this value, as the standard (see Form 10.2). The behavioral plan requires the child to be in his seat for that period of time to earn several minutes of out-of-seat time *right after that interval*. If the child stays in his seat for 4 minutes, he immediately gets 4 minutes of out-of-seat time. However, if the child gets up before the 4-minute interval is over, he is brought back to his seat and the timer is reset to 4 minutes. Once the child reliably achieves the standard, the teacher can gradually increase the in-seat interval required. Concurrently, the teacher also begins decreasing the out-of-seat time that is earned.

TERMS

Premack Principle a behavior of high probability can be used to reinforce a behavior of lower probability (Premack, 1959, 1965).

average interval of in-seat behavior the average (mean) length of time children are able to stay in their seats over a period of time. It is calculated by dividing the length of the period (e.g., 60 minutes) by the number of times the child gets out of the seat (e.g., 12, which would yield a 5-minute average interval of in-seat behavior).

in-seat standard the length of time the child must remain in seat (continuously) to be allowed out-of-seat for a designated period of time.

APPARATUS

The apparatus needed for this program is an oven timer that can be reset. It can be placed on the child's desk or on the teacher's desk.

BASELINE MEASUREMENT

The teacher needs to determine the average length of in-seat behavior for the target child. As delineated previously, he must record the frequency of out-of-seat behavior during a specific designated period (e.g., 10–11 A.M.). He then divides the frequency of out-of-seat behavior into the length of time (e.g., 10 out-of-seat occurrences in 60 minutes yields an average in-seat interval of 6 minutes). The teacher, to compute an accurate estimate of the in-seat interval, immediately sits the child back in his or her seat when the child gets up. The teacher does this for a 6-day baseline period. A chart like the one shown in Figure 10.1 will help the teacher collect and record this data.

PROCEDURES

1. Identify the target child.
2. Collect 6 to 8 days of baseline data in the target class period(s).
3. Set the initial in-seat standard by computing the average interval of in-seat behavior across the designated time period (that is, the number of out-of-seat occurrences divided into the duration of the class period). Use this value to determine the initial in-seat standard, setting an oven timer for that amount.
4. Tell the child that he must remain in his seat for the length of time that the oven timer is set (see Form 10.3).
5. If the child gets out of seat before the timer rings, redirect the child back to his seat and *reset* the timer for the full in-seat standard time period.
6. If the child achieves the in-seat standard, praise the child and allow the child a designated period of time to be out-of-seat (usually a few minutes). Repeat this process of setting an in-seat interval and giving the child out-of-seat time when he is successful.
7. Once the child conforms to the initial in-seat standard for several days in a row, increase the in-seat interval by a minute or two (see Form 10.4).
8. Continue adjusting the in-seat standard while gradually decreasing the earned out-of-seat time period until the in-seat interval reaches

	Child <u>Sarah K.</u> Time Period <u>10 to 11</u> A.M.			
Date	Number of Out-of-Seat Occurrences	Total	Length of Period	Average In-Seat Interval
1. 3/5	LH1 I	6	24	4 min
2. 3/8	LH1 IIII	9	27	3 min
3. 3/9	LH1	5	20	4 min
4. 3/10	LH1 LH1	10	25	2.5 min
5. 3/11	LH1 I	6	30	5 min
6. 3/12	LH1 III	8	24	3 min

FIGURE 10.1
Baseline of In-Seat Interval

the desired goal (e.g., 20 minutes), depending on the child's age or grade level.

HOW IT WORKS

A specific plan is needed for many children entering the elementary grades who have not acquired the skill of sitting for a long period of time. Often, teacher efforts to develop this skill fail because their expected standard far exceeds the child's ability. For example, children who generally cannot sit for longer than 3 to 5 minutes are required to sit continuously for 25 minutes during a class assignment to receive reinforcement. They never acquire the ability to sit continuously for a designated period of time, making teaching them a more difficult proposition as they get older. In-seat behavior should be addressed early in the child's educational life. This individual management plan can be tailored to teach each child how to remain in-seat for longer and longer periods of time.

Using out-of-seat time to reinforce children for staying in their seats for a designated period of time gives this program its power to gradually develop in-seat behavior. As children stay in their seats for a designated period of time, being out-of-seat becomes a more potent reinforcer and thus a powerful reward for staying in-seat. As the child becomes competent at remaining in-seat, even for a relatively short time (for example, 4 minutes), the teacher can develop the desired level of in-seat capability (e.g., 25 minutes) by gradually increasing the in-seat standard (from 4 to 6 minutes, then to 8 minutes, and so on).

The use of out-of-seat time as the reinforcer for achieving the in-seat standard exemplifies a basic principle in behavior analysis called the Premack Principle (Premack, 1959, 1965). For example, playing with friends after school is a higher probability event (i.e., more preferred) than doing homework for most children. The Premack Principle arranges a temporal conditional relationship between engaging in the less preferred activity (doing homework) and then earning the more preferred activity (going out to play). Another example of the Premack Principle would making more preferred academic tasks (e.g., computer learning games) conditional upon the completion of a lesser preferred task (e.g., seat-work assignment).

ADDITIONAL CONSIDERATION

Implementing the Program with One Student at a Time

Because this program requires intensive intervention and supervision by the teacher, the teacher may want to institute this program with only one child at a time. Therefore, if several children in the class lack the skill of staying in their seat, consider implementing it with only one or possibly two children at a time. To attempt to implement this individualized program across many children at once would be extremely time consuming, and additional personnel and resources would probably be needed. However, the simplicity of this program lends itself well to being implemented by noncertificated personnel in inclusive environments.

HYPOTHETICAL EXAMPLE: INCREASING SITTING DURING STORY TIME

Miss Haratio has identified several kindergarten students who have difficulty listening to a story for 10 minutes at a time. She decides to implement this program with each student individually. If this program is successful with the first child, she will implement the plan with the others. Miss Haratio sees that Tanicia gets up during story time about 5 times in a 10-minute period. That is a 2-minute average sitting time.

All the children have carpet squares and are expected to sit in the carpet square while the teacher reads the story to the class. Miss Haratio informs Tanicia that a timer will be set for 2 minutes. If she can remain on the carpet square for 2 continuous minutes, she may get up and stand by Miss Haratio for a short time. However, if Tanicia gets up before the timer goes off, she is not allowed to stand next to Miss Haratio. Rather, she will be required to sit back on the carpet square for an additional 2 minutes. Within a month, Tanicia is able to sit at least 6 continuous minutes before getting up. Building on this success, the teacher plans to use it for the other students who also need help in this area.

WHAT IF?

- Why is out-of-seat time the most powerful reinforcer for children who frequently get out of their seat?
- What are some logistical problems Miss Haratio might face in implementing the program during story time for all the children in the class? What are some possible solutions?
- In what grade level(s) could you envision using this program? What adaptations would be needed for older students?

FORMS

10.1 Baseline Chart of In-Seat Interval—Enables the teacher to calculate the average in-seat interval over several days (can use this data sheet for data collection during Grandma's Rule). Sum up the tally marks, and divide the sum into the length of time.

10.2 Monitoring Sheet for Grandma's Rule—Teacher posts this at the child's desk, specifying the target goal and recording each time the child was able to remain in-seat for the target interval length within the class period.

10.3 Rule Reminder for Student—Teacher posts this for student(s).

10.4 In-Seat Behavior: Teacher-Designated Plan—Teacher uses the form for the written plan.

FORM 10.1

Baseline Chart of In-Seat Interval

Child: _____

Date	Number of Out-of-Seat Occurrences	Total	Length of Period	Average In-Seat Interval
1.				
2.				
3.				
4.				
5.				
6.				
7.				
8.				

———— **FORM 10.2** ————

Monitoring Sheet for Grandma's Rule

Child: _____

Date: _____

Period: _____

Target in-seat standard: _____

Tally number of times child meets the previous in-seat standard during the period:

Tally: _____   Total: _____

FORM 10.3

Rule Reminder for Student

Rule: Stay in your seat until the timer goes off. Ask the teacher for permission to leave your seat when the timer goes off.

<u>You have earned time off.</u>

FORM 10.4

In-Seat Behavior: Teacher-Designated Plan

Child: _____

Target behavior(s): <u>Continuous in-seat behavior</u>

Designated class period(s): _____

Baseline data across five times/sessions (designate average in-seat interval):

Days   1. _____

         2. _____

         3. _____

         4. _____

         5. _____

Initial in-seat standard: _____

Criteria for adjusting in-seat standard up: _____

Criteria for adjusting in-seat standard down: _____

Length of time the child is allowed out-of-seat (if in-seat standard is achieved): _____

_____

Rules for out-of-seat time: _____

Parental consent (if needed): _____

Administrator signature (if needed): _____

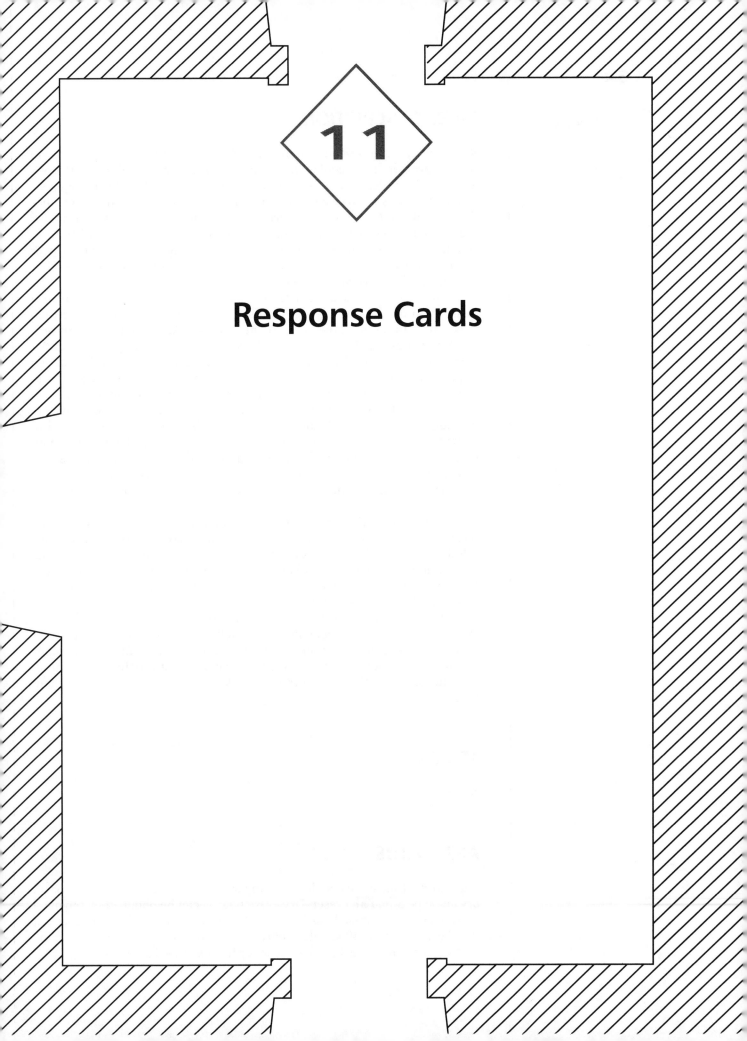

11

Response Cards

BRIEF DESCRIPTION

Research has demonstrated that student engagement is a major factor in the achievement and acquisition of material (Bickel & Bickel, 1986; Brophy & Good, 1986; Kerr & Nelson, 1993; McLaughlin, 1984). In many classrooms, teachers present curriculum content without determining whether the students understand the material. The teacher may present material for a 20-minute period, for example, without assessing each student's understanding of the content. One must realize that calling on one child to answer a question does not enable the teacher to accurately monitor how the other students in the class would respond.

The "response card" technique enables the teacher to present oral instruction or seat-work assignments for short periods of time and then check the students' knowledge of the content (Armendariz & Umbreit, 1999; Cavanaugh, Heward, & Donelson, 1996; Christie & Schuster, 2003; Gardner et al., 1994; Narayan et al., 1990). This technique can be likened to periodic "teach-test-teach-test" instructional models. The teacher presents a certain amount of material then poses a series of questions to all the students. The students respond by writing two- to three-word answers on their dry erase boards and presenting their answers upon a signal to show their work. The teacher surveys all the answers, picking up which students may be unclear about the material or readings. In contrast to selecting one student at a time to answer, the teacher can determine whether most of the students have acquired the skills being taught using this technique.

For example, with a reading assignment, the teacher may designate the pages the students are to read within a certain amount of time. When they are done, the teacher poses questions about the content and the students are given a few seconds to respond using their dry erase boards. At the teacher's signal, the students show their answers and the teacher scans the class, checking each student's answer.

The response card system requires a fair amount of extra work by the teacher or curriculum specialist. The teacher identifies the broad content area to be presented and then divides this material into small "teachable" chunks. The teacher generates a number of questions for each chunk that measure whether students learned what the teacher intended them to learn.

TERMS

None.

APPARATUS

Each student must have a clear writing surface, such as a dry erase board, dry erase pen, and an eraser. Dry erase boards can be obtained by buying a large sheet of dry erase board at a hardware store and having the store cut the sheet into 30 or 40 smaller boards. Other surfaces can be used, but the writing needs to be visible to the teacher from several feet away.

The teacher also needs to generate test items or questions for each chunk of the instructional material. The teacher might also "wing it" and present items once he has presented the small pieces of the topic or content area.

PROCEDURES

1. Identify the content or class period in which the response card system will be used and the chunks of material to be presented.
2. Give each student a dry erase board and a dry erase pen.
3. Explain the response card system to the students.
4. Present the chunk of material or the assignment.
5. Ask a question after the presentation of the material or completion of the assignment.
6. Give the students a few seconds to write their answers on their dry erase boards, then signal them to show their answers.
7. Scan the class, praising students (a few) who gave the correct answer and present the correct answer to the class.
8. If several students made errors, present the item again.
9. Ask additional questions until the presentation has been adequately assessed.

HOW IT WORKS

This method is effective in engaging students in the instructional content via a written or oral presentation. It can be used in areas such as math, oral reading, language arts, science, spelling, and social studies. Because of the need for the students to write their responses, it may not be appropriate for kindergarten and some first-grade students (except for math problems). It is an effective instructional tool as well as a system to increase students' attention to orally presented instruction or reading assignments done in class.

This excerpt demonstrates teacher-presented content followed by instructional questions to which the students respond on the dry erase board:

(Teacher presentation) Today, let's discuss how to add like fractions. As you can see on the board, I have the problem $1/3 + 1/3$. These are like fractions in that the bottom number is the same in both fractions—that is, 3. When the bottom number is the same, in adding fractions you merely add the top numbers. In this case, $1 + 1$. You get the answer $1/3 + 1/3 = 2/3$.

Test question: What is $1/4 + 1/4$? *Begin!* (students write down the answer). Ready, show (students show their answers, with the teacher scanning the class to check everyone's answers). Okay, good. Let's try this one. What is $1/3 + 2/3$? *Begin!* (students write down their answers). Ready, show (students show their answers). Test question: Write a like fraction. *Begin!* (students write down their answers). Ready, show (students show their answers, indicating that the bottom numbers of the fractions are the same).

ADDITIONAL CONSIDERATION

Designing Test Items for "Chunks"

If the same textbooks are used for certain content areas across a number of classroom grades, it might be useful for a school district to assemble a team of curriculum planners who would design the test items for specific instructional chunks. These test items could be made available to all teachers teaching in that area. For example, a set of test items for each chunk could be developed for the adapted seventh-grade social studies book.

HYPOTHETICAL EXAMPLE: USE OF RESPONSE CARDS IN AN ALGEBRA I CLASS

The high school algebra I teacher, Mr. Fernandez, is unhappy with the students' lack of attention during his class lectures. Mr. Fernandez introduces concepts by demonstrating problems and their solutions on the dry erase board at the front of the classroom. He suspects that while he is writing, many students are not observing the demonstration of the process to solve the algebraic problem. Subsequently, when he gives an in-class assignment on that topic, several students raise their hand and say, "I don't understand." Mr. Fernandez contends that such students would understand if they would pay attention while he is teaching instead of text messaging their friends. With algebra I being a required course in the state to pass high school, he does not want his students jeopardizing their educational future. His inability to get some of his students to attend better to instruction is making him frustrated with teaching math in high school.

He decides to use the Response Cards technique he read in a textbook on classroom management. He gets 30 dry erase boards for the 3 algebra I classes he teaches. He considers developing smaller units of instruction so that he may then present test items over each smaller unit he presents in class. As an example, for the unit on graphing basic linear equations, he divides the teaching of this skill into several components. First he will make sure that the students know how to rearrange an equation into slope intercept form (i.e., $y = mx + b$). He presents a few examples of the process on the overhead transparency projector and then presents test items for that skill for all students to answer on their dry erase boards. An example of a test item is the following: "Put this equation into slope intercept form: $3x - y \times 16$." When the students are competent at putting an equation into slope intercept form (e.g., $y = 3x - 16$), he teaches them how to identify the slope of the line and the coordinate points for the y-intercept. Again he teaches to that part of the problem by demonstrating several examples and follows with student responses to several "test" items on the dry erase board (e.g., "In the equation $y = 3x - 16$, what are the coordinate point for the y intercept? Write your answer now.").

Over several weeks, Mr. Fernandez has noted that the students' attention to his instructional presentation has improved drastically. Further, when an in-class or homework assignment is made, few students are unsure of how to solve the problems. He feels that not only has student performance improved, but that his teaching practice has also. While it requires a little advance thought on constructing the format of the "test" items and the specific instructional examples that will be used to demonstrate the math operation, Mr. Fernandez feels it is worth his effort. With pride, he senses he has helped some of his students have hope that they will get a high school diploma and not simply an attendance certificate!

WHAT IF?

Discuss how response cards can be used for the following activities:

- Spelling practice
- Silent reading of history
- Math word problems
- Oral reading
- Language arts lessons
- Think about how this would work for younger students. What test items might you construct for younger students who do not spell well?

Notes

Epilogue

The material in this text provides the user with practical classroom management plans for common problem areas: (a) on-task behavior and assignment completion and (b) disruptive behavior and rule violations. Of course, there are many more plans one could design, but these, and variations thereof, constitute a formidable arsenal of techniques for a teacher to use in the classroom.

Before closing, a few tips and suggestions are offered to the teacher:

1. *Approach the solving of behavior problems with confidence.* Armed with these plans, have the attitude that you can eventually solve a problem. Don't settle for defeat before you begin!

2. *Don't give up too easily.* It may take several variations of your first plan before you find the right combination of procedures. Develop a "don't quit" attitude.

3. *Let data be your guide.* Learn to rely on the analysis of the child's performance to guide your teaching and management strategies.

4. *Realize your importance.* You are often one of the major influences in a child's current and future life. Your role in society is of utmost importance. What you do today can make a difference!

5. *Keep up with the empirical base.* While some research in education may seem as if it has no relevance to everyday teaching (and it may not), the material presented herein does have relevance and it is advanced on the basis of many studies. Consult the journals listed in the references for up-to-data information on effective techniques that have been validated through research findings.

6. *Be an advocate for effective techniques.* When you see others use ineffective techniques, serve as a resource. (See Appendix B.)

Appendix A

USING POWERFUL REINFORCERS IN YOUR CLASSROOM

Many of the plans in this book use point systems. The students earn points for target appropriate behavior, and the points are later traded in for highly preferred events, activities, or tangible items, called "back-up" reinforcers. If the back-up reinforcer is not capable of motivating the student day after day to perform to the level where she or he earns that reinforcer, the management system becomes progressively weaker. Many behavioral plans fail because they do not use reinforcers that are powerful in motivating students, day in and day out.

The power of the back-up reinforcers in any behavioral plan can mean the difference between success and failure. Using weak back-up reinforcers may not generate much student improvement on the targeted behaviors. Altering what is on the reinforcement menu can make all the difference in the world. For example, stickers are often used as the sole reinforcer (i.e., no back-up reinforcer for stickers) by many teachers. While some children may exhibit high levels of work completion for the sole access to a sticker on their paper, they are usually not the children the teacher is having difficulty with in the first place. However, if every sticker they earned bought 2 minutes of extra P.E. time that week, just watch the improvement in most children, who like P.E.

Two almost universal back-up reinforcers available to teachers are extra free time (Zarcone & Fisher, 1996) and break from work (or homework). In some classroom applications, as little as 3 extra minutes was found to be powerful enough to motivate increased performance (N. Erken, personal communication, 1986). This could be done either by releasing those students earlier to recess in the morning and/or afternoon or by having those students not come in until later. Another possibility is releasing them 2 minutes early to head for the school buses (B. Matthew, personal communication, 2002). Matthew reports that getting out early to go home has been used as a powerful contingency. If such is unfeasible every day, the students can accumulate earned extra recess over the course of several days until the exchange is allowed. I must state that I like back-up reinforcers that are available every day, especially for younger students.

Earned breaks from assignments can be taken for either class assignments or homework. A teacher can create many graded variations of these reinforcers:

Extra Recess—Points Needed

- 3 minutes extra lunch recess—5 points
- 4 minutes extra lunch recess—10 points
- 5 minutes extra lunch recess—20 points

Break from Daily Homework—Points Needed

- Break from half of the homework amount—5 points
- Break from entire assignment—20 points

A powerful reinforcer that is available to all teachers is students earning a break from tasks, in the form of break cards (see Cipani, 2004, for greater delineation of the break card program). When one considers that engaging in an instructional task is usually a less preferred activity than a host of other activities, one can see that escaping such a task can become a powerful incentive (Cipani, 1990; Cipani, 1993; Cipani, 1994; Iwata, 1987; Iwata, Vollmer, & Zarcone, 1990). Break cards can be used for both in-class assignments and homework assignments.

Students can earn break cards as a function of the particular management system being deployed in the classroom. For example, in the Good Behavior Board Game several slips of paper can be placed in the treasure box with various amounts of break time written on them, such as 3, 5, 8, or 10 minutes. When the class earns enough break time as a function of drawing slips of paper out of the treasure box, the class can get a free half-period. As another example of using break cards, the student can earn a specific amount of break time as a function of his or her individual behavioral contract. For example, the student may earn 10 minutes of break time for every 3 days she completes all homework assignments.

Break cards are well suited for management systems that use some form of point system. It therefore can also be used when the child earns enough points on the Beeper System. The teacher would have to specify how many points are needed to buy a break card, such as the number of points needed to buy a 5-minute break card. The child can save these break cards and use them when she or he wants an "earned break" from the classroom activity. For example, if the child saves 50 minutes in break cards, she or he can get an entire period off. It can also be used in Behavioral Contracting, and it can be the obtained reinforcer for the Individual Disruptive Incident Barometer.

It is important for the teacher to designate the conditions under which break cards may not be used (e.g., during a test, during presentation of new material, or during other special activities or events). The teacher should delineate in writing those situations or conditions under which the break cards may not be used. The following is a hypothetical chart delineating such situations:

Break Cards May Not Be Used Under the Following Circumstances

1. When I am giving a test.
2. When I am presenting new material to the entire class.

3. When the class has a special activity scheduled.
4. When you have less than 25 minutes of earned break time.

Two methods that are most useful for teachers are: (a) ask the students, and (b) watch what they do.

ASK THE STUDENTS

Ask students what they would like to earn (Northrup, George, Jones, Broussard, & Vollmer, 1996). Get many answers. Some answers may be impractical or unfeasible, either logistically or financially, such as a trip to Hawaii. Write these suggestions down and consider whether such can be earned daily or at the end of the week. Students earning break cards or access to preferred time can have such items or activities during those times.

For example, teenage students like music CDs, videos, teen magazines, sports magazines, and so on. When you have your list of such items, go to garage sales, Goodwill stores, and the like and pick up such items. When you have collected enough of these items, open up your classroom rental store. When the student earns enough break card time or preferred activities time, they could "rent" time with these items.

You should also consider allowing the students to bring such items from home (with you being the ultimate arbiter of appropriateness) for use only during times when such is earned. Make sure you have a safe place to store these items if theft is a concern. It might be wise to put them in a lockbox or trunk so that access to these items occurs with your authorization and supervision only.

Young elementary students will probably suggest coloring activities, art activities, drawing, doodling, and playing computer games. Such activities can be used during earned preferred time in the classroom. Again, access to such activities should be a function of earning break or preferred activity time and under your authorization and supervision. Young children like to play outside. Earning several extra minutes can be a powerful motivating consequence. Don't just give them extra recess time because it is sunny out! Teach them that extra privileges are a function of their behavior.

Secondary students enjoy music, talking to one another, listening to CDs, watching DVDs, and free time. If you teach 5 or 6 class periods a day, you can design the system around each class period. For example, a social studies teacher allows the students in each period to earn up to 5 minutes of break from work, to be taken the following day at the end of class. You can also set up a longer term reinforcer. Any student who earns 7 of 9 possible breaks in a 2-week period gets to choose their seat assignment activity on the given Friday.

OBSERVE THEM

You need to be an astute observer of student preferences. While asking the students to delineate possible reinforcing items is certainly helpful, some unique reinforcers may not come to their mind. Watching them will provide you with additional information on student preferences. For example, one afternoon while I was waiting in the front office to do an in-service at an elementary school, I noticed an amazing phenomenon. When the bell signaled the end of the school day, hordes of children ran to this pencil machine and began inserting coins into it as if it were a slot machine in Las Vegas. I asked the principal about the reason for such interest in pencils. He remarked that because the machine produced a pencil with a Pac Man insignia every 6–8 pencils, the children just could not wait to put their money in until they obtained the desired prize. What if this ritual required points? How much behavior change could this generate? Always be on the lookout for the next powerful reinforcer.

Another exemplary illustration of using this method for identifying potential reinforcing activities was reported to me by Kathy, one of my graduate students in the early 1980s. Kathy worked as an instructional aide in a school for severely emotionally disturbed children. Her class already had a token system for student performance and behavior, but she and the teacher were always on the lookout for new items and activities to enhance their system. One day, one of the students brought a bag of marbles to school. He subsequently dropped the bag of marbles during lunch recess in the playground. You can imagine what happened next. To say there was a mad scramble for the marbles is probably an understatement. Many marbles were recovered, but not all. The frenzied scuffling as the children dove for the marbles probably forced some of them into the dirt.

After that day a small but consistent group of children continued hunting for the lost marbles. Sometimes, one of the children would find a marble during this treasure hunt and announce his or her prized catch. The intermittent reinforcement of the children's hunting probably increased their desire to hunt during every recess.

Noting this newfound proclivity for sifting through dirt, Kathy suggested a unique idea. Allowing children to hunt for marbles could be placed on the point system, to be used as a reinforcer. While not all children wanted to buy this reinforcer with their points, the true "treasure hunters" were willing to spend for such a pleasure. I surmise that the teacher and Kathy found a reinforcer that motivated these students for weeks hence. When you see children frequently doing something, given an opportunity to engage in a variety of activities, think reinforcer!

ONE MORE WORD ON REINFORCEMENT

A teacher can have a powerful reinforcement system by using events and activities that the students prefer and are not required to earn. For example, an elementary school and the PTA purchased a jungle gym for $33,000. If it is placed in the yard where everyone has access to it, then the school loses a powerful reinforcer to strengthen appropriate behavior. If it is placed behind a fenced gate, only students who meet some behavioral criteria could be allowed access to it (provided the PTA consents to its use in this manner). Any student who breaks one of the major school rules on a given day does not get the jungle gym pass for the next 24-hour period from his or her teacher.

If many to most teachers in an entire school would be interested in developing classroom management systems for use in their classes, perhaps a special room could be built for a host of fun activities. Many junior high and high school students like to go to arcades. Suppose a room full of games and play stations were available, not for recess but for earned special time. Think how much motivation that would develop. Just make sure that access to such a room is contingent on earning points via the Beeper System, Task Engagement Program, or Good Behavior Board Game. Be on guard for people who want to make it a noncontingent access, meaning that everyone gets access to it. Such a policy would render its use as a reinforcer ineffectual.

May the force of positive reinforcement be with you!

Appendix B

PROVIDING BEHAVIORAL CONSULTATION TO SCHOOL PERSONNEL

Special education personnel and school psychologists are frequently asked to consult on individual cases involving students with behavioral problems in special education and/or inclusive settings. This can occur informally during interactions in the staff break room or more formally as part of a student study team. While it is not the intent of this material to present a comprehensive treatment of behavioral consultation, I feel that some attention to consulting with other school personnel on children with classroom behavior problems is warranted. For a more complete discussion of behavioral consultation the reader is referred to other material (Cipani, 1985, 1999). This section will address how the knowledge of the management plans contained in this text can be used as a consultant.

PROVIDING CONSULTATION (NOT ADVICE-GIVING) ON INDIVIDUAL CASES

While it is often the tendency of many consultants to offer suggestions "on the spot," there is considerable risk to such a process. What happens in many of these circumstances is what I refer to as "advice-giving." The following is a hypothetical scenario depicting this phenomenon:

General Ed teacher: Barbara, have I got a case for you. I have a child who is probably ADHD. He is restless all the time, constantly on the go. For example, he gets out of his seat, and he seems to not be aware of the fact that he is out of his seat. I point that out to him, "Do you realize that you are out of your seat?" He then offers a sincere apology and goes back to his seat. But 10 minutes later he is out of his seat again. While he is not extremely disruptive when he is out of his seat, it is the countless number of incidents each day that are bothersome. He does it over 30 times per day.

Advice giver: Have you tried talking to his mother? I have heard these things are genetic. Maybe you will find out that she also is restless and maybe ADHD herself. Also, I think you should consider testing him for Alzheimer's. He seems to forget that he got out of his seat. Maybe he is the first Alzheimer's case at his early age. Finally, I think time-out might be helpful as a consequence unless he does have Alzheimer's, in which case he won't remember what he did to get placed in time-out.

What is wrong with this approach? It is the same thing that is wrong with mental health professionals who provide advice over the radio (or TV) after a caller relates his or her problems. The radio expert has no quantifiable verification of the problem, the extent of the problem, and whether the problem reported encumbers the entire context of the problem. One takes for granted that the reporting of the problem presents all the details needed to solve the problem. Further, the recommendation of an intervention (e.g., time-out), even if the problem delineation is correct, may not be wise. The "expert" has no knowledge of the listener's ability to carry out the intervention with integrity.

Consultation should involve a more extensive study of the problem and the context before proposing solutions. Effective intervention requires a process that includes: (a) data collection on the reported problem, (b) problem identification and setting of target objectives, in order of priority, (c) consideration of potential strategies that address target objectives, (d) selection of a strategy or strategies, and (e) evaluation of the efficacy of the strategy(ies) by the consultant.

I believe the following steps reduce the likelihood of a consultation failing to solve the problem:

- Collect baseline data.
- Designate the target consultation objective(s).
- Select a plan that addresses the target objective and is ecologically feasible.
  - If task engagement or on-task behavior is the problem (as verified by baseline data), consider designing an individual behavior plan from part 3.
  - If some form of disruptive behavior is the primary problem (as verified by baseline data), consider designing an individual behavior plan from part 2.
- Implement the plan with requisite staff training.
- Evaluate efficacy of plan across time and change plan as needed.

COLLECT BASELINE DATA

"I don't have time for that. I need something right now to fix this problem!" This is a common response to a request for collecting baseline data, particularly from teachers who have had minimal contact or experience with behavioral consultation services. Such teachers are often used to dealing with advice givers. They go and try part or all of the advice without the necessity for collecting baseline data. When it fails, they hunt for another advice giver. What is missing in advice-giving is the clear identification of the target problem and the collection of baseline data that indicates the extent of the problem. Baseline data provide a specific quantitative measurement regarding the extent (frequency) of the problem behavior.

The importance of collecting baseline data cannot be overstressed to the teacher or instructional assistant. If there is resistance to collecting baseline data even after a clear delineation of the necessity, perhaps "half a loaf of bread is better than no bread at all." Possibly as the consultant, you may want to compromise and have baseline data collected for only a portion of the school day. Your intervention can then relate to that period of time as well. If success is achieved, it will not take long for the teacher to want to extend the program.

Almost all the behavioral plans in this text require baseline data prior to implementation. The baseline data form is usually included in the forms section of each plan.

DESIGNATE THE TARGET CONSULTATION OBJECTIVE(S)

The selection of the target behavioral objective designates which behaviors will be targeted for direct intervention. The selection of the target behavior should result from the baseline data. If on-task behavior were being measured, the target objective would designate an increase of that behavior over the baseline rate. Similarly, if some form of disruptive behavior were being measured, the same form of disruptive behavior would be designated as the consultation objective (in the form of a decrease).

In some cases, the baseline data may reveal that the rate of the measured behavior is not at problematic levels. An intervention set up for that behavior would not have resolved the consultee's woes. In such cases, it is possible that some other behavior may be at the heart of the problem. An advice giver would not be able to detect such because an intervention was designated without verifying the extent of the referred problem. Collecting baseline data will allow the consultant to focus directly on the problem causing the consternation of the referral source.

SELECT A PLAN THAT ADDRESSES TARGET OBJECTIVE AND IS ECOLOGICALLY FEASIBLE

The plans designed in this book fall into two general categories: (a) plans for increasing on-task and assignment completion, and (b) plans for decreasing disruptive behavior. Depending on the nature of the consultation objectives, a plan is selected that addresses the target objective from part 2 or part 3. The selection of a plan that is ecologically feasible requires consideration from the consultant.

If you "run" your own classroom, your selection of one of these management plans automatically accounts for a "good fit." For example, the

Beeper System is a well-designed management system that produces changes in student on-task behavior across an entire class. For some teachers, it is perfect, given their need to change on-task behavior and the number of students in their class. For other teachers, however, its use may not be straightforward. For some teachers with large classes, the requisite frequent monitoring of on-task behavior via the signal may be unfeasible (not a good fit). Perhaps monitoring groups of students may be easier, or increasing the length of time between signals should be considered. Maybe the TEP program would be more feasible than the Beeper System. As a consultant, you should survey the context and gain a sense of whether a certain intervention is practical.

IMPLEMENT PLAN WITH REQUISITE STAFF TRAINING

An advice giver simply tells the listener what to do. How many times have you heard this advice; "Just ignore the behavior. she will stop soon." How many times have you witnessed the receiver of that advice report back that the advice was ineffective? What is at fault: the procedure (ignoring) or the implementation? The answer: You do not know!

Hopefully you have gained a fine appreciation for the detail involved in classroom management plans. In contrast, advice giving leaves a lot to the imagination of the listener. For example, considering the above advice, what would be your understanding? Should the teacher ignore all inappropriate behavior? Should the teacher pay attention to all good behavior? Should the teacher ignore the behavior if the child runs out of the classroom? Hits another child? Should the teacher ignore the child by simply turning away, or is it acceptable to tell the child that as long as he behaves that way, he will not get your attention? As you can see, a lot is left to the imagination.

At a minimum, didactic instruction should be given to the consultee. This can involve written material, such as a copy of the plan from this book, and face-to-face discussion of the procedures. If at all possible, follow up your didactic training with direct observation of the teacher's implementation in the classroom. In that manner, you may conference with the teacher about his or her implementation as well as about problems with logistics. If the plan implementation is not a good fit, perhaps direct observation may reveal how it can be altered to be more feasible for the particular classroom. I have received calls from people who have used these plans with success. Invariably, they mentioned that some revision had been required.

EVALUATE EFFICACY OF PLAN ACROSS TIME AND CHANGE PLAN AS NEEDED

A second purpose for baseline data is to allow for a comparison between what the level of problem behavior was before and after the intervention. To evaluate the efficacy of a plan, one needs a basis for comparison, which baseline data provides. Again, this cannot be overstressed to the consultee in the attempt to get him or her to collect baseline data. On the other hand, advice giving does not provide the basis for comparison, which is another reason for consultants to avoid such a practice.

The collection of data before and after intervention allows the consultant and consultee to also consider if revisions to the plan need to be made. Revisions to the plan are based on weeks of data, not on the crisis that occurred yesterday. Too often without the basis for comparison, effective plans are dropped when one "bad day" occurs, simply because of failure to compare the long-term rates of the behavior before and after intervention. Periodic crises should not result in an alteration of the plan with each crisis. As an example, the Disruptive Incident Barometer should not be dropped as a result of the student having 2 consecutive days in which she failed to earn the daily reinforcer. The long-term comparison may reveal that the plan has reduced the rate from baseline by 50%. What is needed in this hypothetical circumstance is perspective regarding the long-term efficacy.

In summary, these plans can help during consultations with other personnel. But realize that a careful approach to providing behavioral consultation should be taken. The effective use of these plans by others often depends on it. A format for a progress summary you may find helpful in evaluating your intervention periodically appears on page 177.

Progress Summary

Date: _____

Child: _____

Baseline rate: _____

Current rate: _____

Progress toward objective:　　Yes　　No

Maintain current plan:　　Yes　　No

Revise current plan:　　Yes　　No

References

Abramowitz, A. J., & O'Leary, S. G. (1991). Behavioral interventions for the classroom: Implications for students with ADHD. *School Psychology Review, 20*, 220–234.

Alberto, P. A., & Troutman, A. C. (2006). *Applied behavior analysis for teachers* (7th ed.). Upper Saddle River, NJ: Merrill/Prentice Hall.

Ardoin, S. P., Martens, B. K., & Wolfe, L. A. (1999). Using high-probability request sequences with fading to increase student compliance during transitions. *Journal of Applied Behavior Analysis, 32*, 339–351.

Armendariz, F., & Umbreit, J. (1999). Using active responding to reduce disruptive behavior in a general education classroom. *Journal of Positive Behavioral Interventions, 1*, 152–158.

Ayllon, T., & Robert, M. D. (1974). Eliminating discipline problems by strengthening academic performance. *Journal of Applied Behavior Analysis, 7*, 71–76.

Baer, D. M., Wolf, M. M., & Risley, T. R. (1968). Some current dimensions of applied behavior analysis. *Journal of Applied Behavior Analysis, 1*, 91–97.

Bailey, J. S., & Burch, M. R. (2002). *Research methods in applied behavior analysis*. Thousand Oaks, CA: Sage Publications.

Barrish, H. H., Saunders, M., & Wolf, M. M. (1969). Good behavior game: Effects of individual contingencies for group consequences on disruptive behavior in a classroom. *Journal of Applied Behavior Analysis, 2*, 119–124.

Becker, W. C., Madsen, C. H., Arnold, C. R., & Thomas, D. R. (1967). The contingent use of teacher attention and praising in reducing classroom problems. *Journal of Special Education, 1*, 287–307.

Bickel, W. E., & Bickel, D. D. (1986). Effective schools, classrooms, and instruction: Implications for special education. *Exceptional Children, 52*, 489–500.

Bolstad, O. D., & Johnson, S. M. (1972). Self-regulation in the modification of disruptive classroom behavior. *Journal of Applied Behavior Analysis, 5*, 443–454.

Brooks, A., Todd, A., Tofflemoyer, S., & Horner, R. (2003). Use of functional assessment and a self-management system to increase academic engagement and work completion. *Journal of Positive Behavioral Interventions, 5*, 144–152.

Brophy, J., & Good, T. L. (1986). Teacher behavior and student achievement. In M. C. Wittrock (Ed.), *Handbook of research on teaching* (3rd ed., pp. 328–375). Upper Saddle River, NJ: Prentice Hall.

Carpenter, S., & McKee-Higgins, E. (1996). Behavior management in inclusive classrooms. *Remedial and Special Education, 17*, 196–203.

Cavanaugh, R. A., Heward, W. L., & Donelson, F. (1996). Effects of response cards during lesson closure on the academic performance of secondary students in an earth science course. *Journal of Applied Behavior Analysis, 29*, 403–405.

Christie, C. A., & Schuster, J. W. (2003). The effects of response cards on student participation, academic achievement, and on-task behavior during whole-class, math instruction. *Journal of Behavioral Education, 12*, 147–165.

Cipani, E. (1985). The three phases of behavioral consultation: Objectives, intervention, and quality assurance. *Teacher Education and Special Education, 8*, 144–152.

Cipani, E. (1990). The communicative function hypothesis: An operant behavior perspective. *Journal of Behavior Therapy and Experimental Psychiatry, 21*, 239–247.

Cipani, E. (1993). *Non-compliance: Four strategies that work*. Reston, VA: Council for Exceptional Children.

Cipani, E. (1994). Treating children's severe behavior disorders: A behavioral diagnostic system. *Journal of Behavior Therapy and Experimental Psychiatry, 25*, 293–300.

Cipani, E. (1999). *Helping parents help their kids: A clinical guide to six child problem behaviors*. Philadelphia: Brunnel/Mazel.

Cipani, E. (2004). *Classroom management for all teachers: Twelve plans for evidence-based practice*. Upper Saddle River, NJ: Pearson/Merrill Prentice Hall.

Cipani, E., & McLaughlin, T. F. (1983). The effects of contingent re-checking on academic performance. *Corrective and Social Psychology, 29*, 88–93.

Cohen, M. E., & Close, D. W. (1975). Retarded adults' discrete work performance in a sheltered workshop as a function of overall productivity and motivation. *American Journal of Mental Deficiency, 79*, 426–529.

Deci, E. L. (1971). Effects of externally mediated rewards on intrinsic motivation. *Journal of Personality and Social Psychology, 18*, 105–115.

Dietz, S. M., & Repp, A. C. (1973). Decreasing classroom misbehavior through the use of DRL schedules of reinforcement. *Journal of Applied Behavior Analysis, 6*, 457–464.

Drake, R. E., Goldman, H. E., Leff, H. S., Lehman, A. F., Dixon, L., Mueser, K. T., & Torrey, W. C. (2001). Implementing evidence-based practices in routine mental health service settings. *Psychiatric Services, 52*, 179–182.

Ducharme, J. M., & Worling, D. E. (1994). Behavioral momentum and stimulus fading in the acquisition and maintenance of child compliance in the home. *Journal of Applied Behavior Analysis, 27*, 639–647.

DuPaul, G., Guevermont, D., & Barkley, R. (1992). Behavioral treatment of attention-deficit hyperactivity disorder in the classroom. *Behavior Modification, 16*, 204–225.

Erken, N., & Henderson, H. (1989). *Practice skills mastery program*. Logan, UT: Mastery Programs Limited.

Foxx, R. M., & Shapiro, S. T. (1978). The time-out ribbon: A nonexclusionary timeout procedure. *Journal of Applied Behavior Analysis, 11*, 125–136.

Gardner, R., Heward, W. C., & Grossi, T. A. (1994). Effects of response cards on student participation and academic achievement: A systematic replication with inner-city students during whole-class science instruction. *Journal of Applied Behavior Analysis, 27*, 63–71.

Goldfried, M. R., & Davison, G. C. (1976). *Clinical behavior therapy*. New York: Holt, Rinehart & Winston.

Greenwood, C. R., Delquadri, J. C., & Hall, R. V. (1984). *Opportunity to respond and student academic achievement*. In W. L. Heward, T. E. Heron, D. S. Hill, & J. Trap-Porter (Eds.), *Focus on behavior analysis in education* (pp. 58–88). Columbus, OH: Merrill.

Greenwood, C. R., Hops, H., Delquadri, J., & Guild, J. (1974). Group contingencies for group consequences in classroom management: A further analysis. *Journal of Applied Behavior Analysis, 7*, 413–425.

Gunter, P. L., Venn, M. L., Patrick, J., Miller, K. A., & Kelly, L. (2003). Efficacy of using momentary time samples to determine on-task behavior of students with emotional behavioral disorders. *Education and Treatment of Children, 26*, 400–412.

Hall, R. V., Fox, R., Willard, D., Goldsmith, M., Emerson, M., Owen, F., Davis, F., & Porcia, E. (1971). The teacher as observer and experimentor in the modification of disputing and talking-out behaviors. *Journal of Applied Behavior Analysis, 4,* 141–149.

Harris, V. W., Finfrock, S. R., Giles, D. K., Hart, B. M., & Tsosie, P. C. (1975). *The effects of performance contingencies on the assignment completion behavior of severely delinquent youth.* In E. Ramp & G. Semb (Eds.), *Behavior analysis: Areas of research and application* (pp. 309–316). Upper Saddle River, NJ: Prentice Hall.

Harris, V. W., & Sherman, J. A. (1973). Use and analysis of the "good behavior game" to reduce disruptive classroom behavior. *Journal of Applied Behavior Analysis, 6,* 405–417.

Henderson, H. S., Jenson, W. R., Erken, N. R., Davidsmeyer, P. L., & Lampe, S. (1986). Variable interval reinforcement as a practical means of increasing and maintaining on-task behavior in classrooms. *Education and Treatment of Children, 9,* 250–263.

Higgins, J. W., Williams, R. L., & McLaughlin, T. F. (2001). The effects of a token economy employing instructional consequences for a third-grade student with learning disabilities: A data-based case study. *Education and Treatment of Children, 24,* 99–107.

Homme, L. E. (1970). *How to use contingency contracting.* Champaign, IL: Research Press.

Hopkins, B. C., Schutte, R. C., & Garton, K. C. (1971). The effects of access to a playroom on the rate and quality of printing and writing of first- and second-grade students. *Journal of Applied Behavior Analysis, 4,* 77–87.

Inkster, A., & McLaughlin, T. F. (1993). Token reinforcement: Effects for reducing tardiness with a socially disadvantaged adolescent student. *B. C. Journal of Special Education, 17,* 176–182.

Iwata, B. A. (1987). Negative reinforcement in applied behavior analysis: An emerging technology. *Journal of Applied Behavior Analysis, 20,* 361–378.

Iwata, B. A., Bailey, J. S., Brown, K. M., Foshee, T. J., & Alpert, M. (1976). A performance-based lottery to improve residential care and training by institutional staff. *Journal of Applied Behavior Analysis, 9,* 417–431.

Iwata, B., Dorsey, M., Slifer, K., Bauman, K., & Richman, G. (1994). Toward a functional analysis of self-injury. *Journal of Applied Behavior Analysis, 27,* 197–209. (Reprint of original article published in *Analysis and Intervention in Developmental Disabilities, 2,* 3–20.)

Iwata, B. A., Vollmer, T. R., & Zarcone, J. H. (1990). The experimental (functional) analysis of behavior disorders: Methodology, applications, and limitations. In A. C. Repp & N. N. Singh (Eds.), *Current perspectives in nonaversive and aversive interventions with developmentally disabled persons* (pp. 301–330). Sycamore, IL: Sycamore Publishing.

Jackson, G. M. (1979). The use of visual orientation feedback to facilitate attention and task performance. *Mental Retardation, 27,* 281–304.

Jones, F. H. (1987). *Positive classroom discipline.* New York: McGraw-Hill.

Kaufman, K. E., & O'Leary, K. D. (1972). Reward, cost, and self-evaluation procedures for disrutpive adolescents in a psychiatric hospital school. *Journal of Applied Behavior Analysis, 5,* 293–309.

Kazdin, A. E. (1977). *The token economy: A review and evaluation.* New York: Plenum Press.

Kazdin, A. E., & Bootzin, R. R. (1972). The token economy: An evaluative review. *Journal of Applied Behavior Analysis, 5,* 343–372.

Kazdin, A. E., & Klock, J. (1973). The effects of nonverbal teacher approval on student attentive data. *Journal of Applied Behavior Analysis, 6,* 643–654.

Kelly, M. L., & Stokes, T. F. (1982). Contingency contracting with disadvantaged youths: Improving classroom performance. *Journal of Applied Behavior Analysis, 15,* 447–454.

Kennedy, C., Meyer, K., Knowles, T., & Shulka, S. (2000). Analyzing the multiple functions of stereotypic behavior for students with autism. *Journal of Applied Behavior Analysis, 33,* 559–571.

Kennedy, C. H., Itkonen, T., & Lindquist, K. (1995). Comparing interspersed instructions and social comments as antecedents for increasing student compliance. *Journal of Applied Behavior Analysis, 28,* 97–98.

Kern, L., Montegna, M., Vorndran, C., Bailin, D., & Hilt, A. (2001). Choice of task sequence to reduce problem behaviors. *Journal of Positive Behavioral Interventions. 3,* 3–10.

Kerr, M. M., & Nelson, C. M. (1993). *Strategies for managing behavior problems in the classroom* (2nd ed.). Upper Saddle River, NJ: Merrill/Prentice Hall.

Kohn, A. (1993). *Punished by rewards: The trouble with gold stars, incentive plans, A's, praise.* Boston: Houghton Mifflin.

Lau, W., & Cipani, E. (1984). Reducing student food waste in a cafeteria-style dining room through contingency management. *Child Care Quarterly, 12,* 301–308.

Mace, F. C., Hock, M. L., Lalli, J. S., West, B. J., Belfiore, P., Pinter, E, & Brown, D. K. (1988). Behavioral momentum in the treatment of noncompliance. *Journal of Applied Behavior Analysis, 21,* 123–141.

Madsen, C. H., Jr., Becker, W. C., & Thomas, D. R. (1968). Rules, praise, and ignoring: Elements of elementary classroom control. *Journal of Applied Behavior Analysis, 1,* 139–150.

Main, G. C., & Munro, B. C. (1977). A token reinforcement program in a public junior high school. *Journal of Applied Behavior Analysis, 10,* 93–94.

McGinnis, J. C., Friman, P. C., & Carlyon, W. D. (1999). The effect of token rewards on "intrinsic" motivation for doing math. *Journal of Applied Behavior Analysis, 32,* 375–379.

McLaughlin, T., & Malaby, J. (1972). Reducing and measuring inappropriate verbalizations in a token classroom. *Journal of Applied Behavior Analysis, 5,* 329–333.

McLaughlin, T. F. (1983). Effects of self-recording for on-task and academic responding: A long term analysis. *Journal for Special Education Technology, 5*(3), 5–12.

McLaughlin, T. F. (1984). A comparison of self-recording and self-recording plus consequences for on-task and assignment completion. *Contemporary Educational Psychology, 9,* 185–192.

Medland, M. B., & Stachnik, T. J. (1972). Good-behavior game: A replication and systematic analysis. *Journal of Applied Behavior Analysis, 5,* 45–51.

Millenson, M. L. (1997). *Demanding medical excellence.* Chicago: University of Chicago Press.

Miller, A. (1996). *Pupil behavior and teacher culture.* New York: Cassell.

Miller, D. L., & Kelley, M. L. (1994). The use of goal setting and contingency contracting for improving children's homework performance. *Journal of Applied Behavior Analysis, 27,* 73–85.

Murphy, J. J. (1988). Contingency contracting in the schools: A review. *Education and Treatment of Children, 11,* 257–269.

Narayan, J. S., Heward, W. L., Gardner, R., Courson, F. H., & Omness, C. K. (1990). Using response cards to increase student participants in an elementary classroom. *Journal of Applied Behavior Analysis, 23,* 483–490.

O'Leary, K. D., & Becker, W. C. (1967). Behavior modification of an adjustment class: A token reinforcement program. *Exceptional Children, 33,* 637–642.

O'Leary, K. D., Becker, W. C., Evans, M. B., & Saudargas, R. A. (1969). A token reinforcement program in a public school: A replication and systematic anaylsis. *Journal of Applied Behavior Analysis, 2,* 3–13.

O'Leary, K. D., & Drabman, R. (1971). Token reinforcement programs in the classroom: A review. *Psychological Bulletin, 75,* 379–398.

O'Leary, K. D., & O'Leary, S. G. (1977). *Classroom management: The successful use of behavior modification* (2nd ed.). New York: Pergamon Press.

Pfiffner, L. J., & O'Leary, S. G. (1987). The efficacy of all-positive management as a function of the prior use of negative consequences. *Journal of Applied Behavior Analysis, 20,* 265–271.

Pfiffner, L. J., Rosen, L. A., & O'Leary, S. G. (1985). The efficacy of an all-positive approach to classroom management. *Journal of Applied Behavior Analysis, 18,* 257–261.

Pigott, H. E., & Heggie, D. L. (1986). Interpreting the conflicting results of individual versus group contingencies in classrooms: The targeted behavior as a mediating variable. *Child & Family Behavior Therapy, 7,* 1–14.

Prater, M. A., Hogan, S., & Miller, S. R. (1992). Using self-monitoring to improve on-task behavior and academic skills of an adolescent with mild handicaps across special and regular education settings. *Education and Treatment of Children, 15,* 43–55.

Premack, D. (1965). *Reinforcement theory.* In D. Levine (Ed.), Nebraska Symposium on Motivation. Lincoln: University of Nebraska Press.

Repp, A. C., Barton, L. E., & Brulle, A. R. (1983). A comparison of two procedures for programming the differential reinforcement of the behaviors. *Journal of Applied Behavior Analysis, 16,* 435–445.

Siagh, P. A., & Umar, A. M. (1983). The effects of a good behavior game on the disruptive behavior of Sudanese elementary school students. *Journal of Applied Behavior Analysis, 16,* 339–344.

Salend, S. J., & Gordon, B. D. (1987). A group-oriented time-out ribbon procedure. *Behavioral Disorders, 12,* 131–137.

Schipp, S. L., Baker, R. J., & Cuvo, A. J. (1980). The relationship between attention to work task and production rate of a mentally retarded client. *Mental Retardation, 18,* 241–243.

Singer, G. H. S., Singer, J., & Horner, R. H. (1987). Using pre-task requests to increase the probability of compliance for students with severe disabilities. *Journal of the Association for Persons with Severe Handicaps, 12,* 287–291.

Speltz, M. L., Wenters-Shimamaura, J., & McReynolds, W. T. (1982). Procedural variations in group contingencies: Effects on children's academic and social behaviors. *Journal of Applied Behavior Analysis, 15,* 533–544.

Swain, J. C., & McLaughlin, T. F. (1998). The effects of bonus contingencies in a classwide token program on math performance with middle school students with behavior disorders. *Behavioral Intervention, 13,* 11–20.

Truhlicka, M., McLaughlin, T. F., & Swain, J. C. (1998). Effects of bonus contingencies and response cost on the accuracy of spelling performance with middle school special education students with behavior disorders. *Behavioral Interventions, 13,* 1–10.

Walker, H. M., Hops, H., & Fiegenbaum, E. (1976). Deviant classroom behavior as a function of combinations of social and token reinforcement and cost contingency. *Behavior Therapy, 7,* 76–88.

Weeks, M., & Gaylord-Ross, R. (1981). Task difficulty and aberrant behavior in severely handicapped students. *Journal of Applied Behavior Analysis, 14,* 449–463.

West, R. P., & Sloane, H. N. (1986). Teacher presentation rate and point delivery rate: Effects on classroom disruption, performance accuracy and response rate. *Behavior Modification, 10,* 267–286.

West, R. P., Young, K. R., Callahan, K., Fister, S., Kemp, K., Preston, J., & Lovitt, T. C. (1995). The musical clocklight: Encouraging positive classroom behavior. *Teaching Exceptional Children, 27,* 46–51.

White, A. G., & Bailey, J. S. (1990). Reducing disruptive behaviors of elementary physical education students with sit and watch. *Journal of Applied Behavior Analysis, 23,* 353–359.

Wolery, M., Bailey, D. B., Jr., & Sugai, G. M. (1988). *Effective teaching principles and procedures of applied behavior analysis with exceptional students.* Boston: Allyn & Bacon.

Yeager, C., & McLaughlin, T. F. (1995). The use of a time-out ribbon and precision requests to improve child compliance in the classroom: A case study. *Child & Family Behavior Therapy, 17,* 1–9.

Zarcone, J. R., & Fisher, W. W. (1996). Analysis of free-time contingencies as positive or negative reinforcement. *Journal of Applied Behavior Analysis, 29,* 247–251.

Zwald, L., & Gresham, F. (1982). Behavioral consultation in a secondary class: Using DRL to decrease negative verbal interactions. *The School Psychology Review, 11*(4), 428–432.